TRANSFORMING

Professional Development

INTO **Student Results**

ASCD MEMBER BOOK

Many ASCD members received this book as a
member benefit upon its initial release.

Learn more at: **www.ascd.org/memberbooks**

TRANSFORMING

Professional
Development

INTO **Student Results**

ASCD

Alexandria, Virginia USA

DOUGLAS B. REEVES

1703 N. Beauregard St. • Alexandria, VA 22311–1714 USA
Phone: 800-933-2723 or 703-578-9600 • Fax: 703-575-5400
Web site: www.ascd.org • E-mail: member@ascd.org
Author guidelines: www.ascd.org/write

Gene R. Carter, *Executive Director;* Nancy Modrak, *Publisher;* Scott Willis, *Director, Book Acquisitions & Development;* Julie Houtz, *Director, Book Editing & Production;* Ernesto Yermoli, *Editor;* Greer Wymond, *Senior Graphic Designer;* Mike Kalyan, *Production Manager;* Valerie Younkin, *Desktop Publishing Specialist;* Kyle Steichen, *Production Specialist*

Printed in the United States of America. Cover art © 2010 by ASCD. ASCD publications present a variety of viewpoints. The views expressed or implied in this book should not be interpreted as official positions of the Association.

All Web links in this book are correct as of the publication date below but may have become inactive or otherwise modified since that time. If you notice a deactivated or changed link, please e-mail books@ascd.org with the words "Link Update" in the subject line. In your message, please specify the Web link, the book title, and the page number on which the link appears.

ASCD Member Book, No. FY10-7 (April, 2010, PSI+). ASCD Member Books mail to Premium (P), Select (S), and Institutional Plus (I+) members on this schedule: Jan., PSI+; Feb., P; Apr., PSI+; May, P; July, PSI+; Aug., P; Sept., PSI+; Nov., PSI+; Dec., P. Select membership was formerly known as Comprehensive membership.

PAPERBACK ISBN: 978-1-4166-0949-0   ASCD product 109050

Also available as an e-book (see Books in Print for the ISBNs).

Quantity discounts for the paperback edition only: 10–49 copies, 10%; 50+ copies, 15%; for 1,000 or more copies, call 800-933-2723, ext. 5634, or 703-575-5634. For desk copies: member@ascd.org.

Library of Congress Cataloging-in-Publication Data
Reeves, Douglas B., 1953–
  Transforming professional development into student results / Douglas B. Reeves.
     p. cm.
  Includes bibliographical references and index.
  ISBN 978-1-4166-0949-0 (pbk. : alk. paper)   1. Teachers—In-service training—United States   2. Teachers—Professional relationships—United States.   3. School improvement programs—United States.   I. Title.
  LB1731.R35 2010
  370.71'55—dc22
                                                                                          2009049912

20 19   18 17 16 15 14 13 12 11 10 09   1 2 3 4 5 6 7 8 9 10 11 12

TRANSFORMING

Professional Development
INTO Student Results

ACKNOWLEDGMENTS

This book benefited from the thoughtful leadership on professional learning provided by several individuals and organizations. In particular, I wish to acknowledge the National Staff Development Council (NSDC) and its visionary leaders, including executive director Stephanie Hirsh and deputy executive director Joellen Killion.

ASCD, the publisher of this book, is an international leader in supporting the distribution of leading-edge research and practice for educators and school leaders. I wish to thank Nancy Modrak, director of publishing; Scott Willis, director of book acquisitions and development; and Ernesto Yermoli, associate editor.

My colleagues at The Leadership and Learning Center were particularly helpful in the research and analysis reported in these pages. I would particularly like to acknowledge Kristin Anderson, Nan Caldwell, Tony Flach, Robin Hoey, Ray Smith, and Stephen White.

Although the reference list at the end of the book acknowledges the many thought leaders who influenced my thinking on this book, I wish to particularly note the prolific advocacy for improved professional learning by Larry Ainsworth, Lisa Almeida, Laura Besser, Rebecca DuFour, Richard DuFour, Robert Eaker, Richard Elmore, Michael Fullan, Daniel Goleman,

Linda Darling-Hammond, Andy Hargreaves, Brian McNulty, Hayes Mizell, and Mike Schmoker.

Cathy Shulkin has devoted almost a decade to editing my work. I fear that her job has not become easier with the passage of time, as my work becomes easier in the same proportion to which hers becomes more difficult. The contribution she makes to each page of this manuscript is immeasurable. The errors, of course, remain my own.

INTRODUCTION
And a Good Time Was Had by All

It has been almost a decade since Guskey (2000) made the case that "Level 1" evaluation of professional learning was inadequate. His clarion call for moving from evaluation based on participant reactions to evaluation based on student learning is among the most important works in the professional development literature. That same year, Jeffrey Pfeffer and Robert Sutton published one of the most influential books of the new century, *The Knowing-Doing Gap* (2000). Both of these books in my library bear the marks of deep respect for the authors—broken spines, turned-down pages, and many scribbled notes.

Educational leaders must now face the reality of the degree to which we have transformed the compelling words of these authors into action. It is seductively easy to remain stuck in Guskey's Level 1, a methodology worthy of the parodies of Sally Fields's acceptance speech at the 1985 Academy Awards ceremony—"They like me! They really like me!" Audience appreciation thus becomes the heroin of professional development, turning otherwise scholarly presenters into sycophantic praise junkies. Just as Gresham's law holds that tainted coins drive pure ones out of circulation, a school's addiction to Level 1 feedback effectively prevents the pursuit of Level 5, as cheap praise prevents us from pursuing strategies that produce great value in improving student learning. Let's call it "Fields's Law of Professional Development," in which the addiction to praise, accompanied by high costs in time, resources, energy, and emotion, drive out hard-won gains in student achievement associated with improved teaching and leadership.

The central challenge for educational systems around the world is the substitution of effectiveness for popularity. *Transforming Professional Development into Student Results* is a guide for teachers, leaders, and policymakers who are willing to take on this challenge. Part 1 describes what is wrong with much of current professional learning. Part 2 provides a blueprint for creating high-impact learning in your professional communities. Part III is designed to help leaders and policymakers at every level sustain high-impact learning over the long term.

What's Wrong with Professional Development?

Part 1 addresses what is wrong with professional development in schools. It is neither an indictment of teachers who are required to endure insufferable PowerPoint presentations nor a criticism of well-intentioned leaders who seek to "train" their colleagues as if they were circus animals. Rather, it is an acknowledgment that good intentions are insufficient to lead to worthwhile professional learning.

We begin in Chapter 1 with a consideration of educational accountability and its transformation from a list of test scores to a learning system for improved decision making and professional practice. The fundamental thesis of effective accountability systems is that our zeal for holding 9-year-old children accountable should be matched by an enthusiasm for assessing the performance of the adults in the system. In the decade since Guskey implored schools to take a more rigorous approach to assessing professional learning, however, accountability is perhaps least in evidence in staff development seminars, as noted in Chapter 2. As we enter the second decade of the millennium full of calls for requiring students to perfect 21st century skills, too many schools remain captivated by staff development experiences that were discredited in previous centuries. Indeed, the critical thinking in the Lyceum of 325 BCE exceeds that of the purveyors of contradictory and evidence-free staff development. Some of those programs allow us to understand the conclusion of Socrates that hemlock might be a blessed relief.

If quality in accountability and assessment is missing from many professional learning efforts, however, it is not for want of quantity. Chapter 3 explores the Law of Initiative Fatigue and the toll that proliferating initiatives have taken on the finances, morale, and organizational energy of school systems. Just as training programs have grown in number if not quality, so have the burdens of planning documents, as discussed in Chapter 4. Although none of these planning requirements have malicious intent, the relationship between school plans and student achievement varies widely. The good news is that some of these requirements are significantly related to improved student results. The bad news is that good leadership actions are crowded out by other planning requirements that have no relationship to improved results. A few cases actually show an inverse relationship—the better the school's compliance with planning requirements, the worse the achievement.

Just as some policymakers have conflated planning documents with effective leadership, others are seduced by brand names and star turns, a situation described in Chapter 5. After tens of millions of dollars have been invested in research on comprehensive school reform models, however, astonishingly little evidence exists to support their effectiveness (Gross, Booker, & Goldhaber, 2009). In fact, the research suggests that the most salient variable in improving student achievement is not the brand name of the program but the degree of implementation of the program. In brief, it is practices and people, not programs, that make the difference for student achievement.

Finally, in Chapter 6 we consider the phenomenon of scattershot learning. Just as Marzano (2001) documented that most states have too many academic standards for the time available in school, staff development catalogs often remain fragmented and unfocused. On the day the manuscript for this book was completed, I reviewed the professional development catalog of a major urban system and found dozens of offerings that were not only inconsistent with the district's stated goals and policies but also inconsistent with each other, providing contradictory advice to teachers and administrators on a range of subjects such as differentiated instruction, assessment, and effective leadership.

How to Fix It

If readers will tolerate the discouragement of Part 1, they will find their persistence rewarded in Part 2, where we explore how to fix what is wrong with professional development in schools. Many school leaders have promising visions of transforming professional learning into action, and Chapter 7 provides practical guidelines for creating a focus on implementation. Applying what we know about effective feedback and assessment in the classroom, leaders can create learning systems for administrators and teachers that provide accurate, specific, and timely feedback. Chapter 8 replaces the laundry list of initiatives with a clear focus on the four imperatives for effective professional learning that are related to student results: teaching, curriculum, assessment, and leadership. It is nearly impossible to overstate the value of focus. As Gallagher (2009) reminds us, focus at the individual and organizational levels offers exceptional rewards, including personal health and well-being and magnified organizational influence.

Our professional landscape is littered with lectures on "critical thinking" that require neither criticism nor thought and orations on "research-based strategies" that are remarkably unburdened by rigorous research. Just as the National Staff Development Council (2009) has wisely established standards for effective professional learning, we can also create standards for research. Chapter 9 suggests that we replace breathless enthusiasm for the latest case study with a commitment to multiple methods, multiple sources, and an abundance of self-deprecation. The publisher of this book, for example, has been willing to print not only success stories but candid accounts of failures, including my own acknowledgment that some of my well-intentioned hypotheses were simply not supported by the evidence (Reeves, 2004a). Research advances not only by confirming prevailing hypotheses but also by challenging them. This is not always an appealing proposition—just ask Galileo. But it is an essential one. That is why this chapter encourages teachers to take an active role not only in expressing hypotheses but also in testing them. Action research has often been stereotyped as the poor second cousin to "real" research, which is distinguished by quantitative methods and experimental designs. But however necessary large-scale quantitative studies may be, legions of teachers engaging in action research can establish the practical application of educational theory. Experimental research and action research are not in opposition to one another; the latter applies the former to the real world of the classroom.

Building Capacity for Long-Term Success

Part 3 considers how to take the lessons of this book and build sustained improvements for schools and educational systems. Chapter 10 challenges the "train the trainer" model that remains widely popular but rarely builds capacity. Thanks to the pioneering work of Ainsworth (2006), DuFour (2008), Stiggins (2004), and Wiggins (1998), we know that "assessment for learning" has a dramatic and positive effect on student achievement. By liberating teachers and students from the burden that every bit of feedback must entail the pronouncement of final judgment, this alternative concept of assessment has refocused feedback from teachers to students and to feedback's central purpose—improved student performance.

Chapter 11 argues that we must practice what we preach, engaging in performance assessment for teachers and school leaders. This is not a call for throwing out existing teacher and administrator evaluations (though that is probably not a bad idea). Rather, it is an argument for distinguishing *evaluation* from *assessment*. Lawyers and human resources professionals run the personnel evaluation system, constrained by collective bargaining agreements and court decisions. Instructional leaders, however, must retain control of assessing teachers and leaders. The former process can be used for dismissing employees who commit felonious assault; the latter can be used to provide feedback to improve performance.

I regularly invite educators and leaders to send me their questions, and hundreds of them do so every month. The most common question, however, is one to which my response is probably most disappointing. The question is "How do I get better buy-in from my staff before I implement some critically needed changes?" The answer is "You don't." This approach flies in the face of the conventional wisdom that places "buy-in" as the essential antecedent of change, but evidence must, at least occasionally, displace conventional wisdom. Chapter 12 concludes the book with the story of high-impact learning in action, based on a real-world synthesis of case studies where these strategies have been applied.

Research Details

To serve the interests of readers who are practitioners, I have largely kept the text clear of the technical details of the research supporting this book. The book is based, in part, on a study by The Leadership and Learning Center of the relationship between how well schools plan, implement, and monitor improvements and how well their students perform in reading and math. The data were gathered from schools in the United States and Canada from 2005 to 2008 based on independent analyses of school planning, implementation, and monitoring processes. Student achievement data were provided by the school systems or secured from publicly available sources, such as the district or state Web sites. Readers who are interested in the research methods, variable definitions, and statistics from the study will find these in the appendices.

Transforming Ideas into Action

The National Staff Development Council (Hirsh, 2009; Wei, Darling-Hammond, Andree, Richardson, & Orphanos, 2009) has led the charge for job-embedded professional learning. Some principals embrace this challenge and are fully prepared for this new level of instructional leadership. Most principals, however, already have a full-time job, and they need a practical method for distributing leadership. The most effective principals understand that custodians, cafeteria workers, bus drivers, and every adult in the system is a teacher through their behavior, their interactions with students and parents, and their specific actions any time they are on the job. They understand that there is a difference between a job that is described as "driving a bus" and one that is described as "caring for the lives of children and getting them safely from their home to school and back."

Superintendents have an overwhelming job, and no amount of intelligence, work ethic, charisma, or political pressure will create a day with more than 24 hours. Every minute spent in pursuit of one priority is another tick of the clock that was not devoted to another priority. In an imperfect world, superintendents must therefore make choices every moment of the day, dispensing with the illusion that multitasking represents effectiveness. Their action plan for high-impact learning does not require the frantic pursuit of more tasks, but rather includes a request that they stop, reconsider, reflect, and reevaluate their professional learning traditions. Telling any superintendent to slow down is, the reader might think, an exercise in futility. Surely my colleagues would say the same about me. But my wise music teacher, David Castillo, reminds me at each lesson, "If you can't go slow, you can't go fast." Professor Castillo's wisdom is supported by a growing body of research on the value of deliberate practice (Coyle, 2009) in fields ranging from music to athletics to leadership.

It is not a dearth of information that is the problem, but our collective failure to translate that information into practical actions. The challenge for school board members and policymakers is not only how to fulfill their legislative mandates to protect the children they are elected to serve, but also to decide what *not* to do. That challenge brings us to where we started—how do we pull the weeds before we plant the flowers? Given the multiplicity of demands on them, how can teachers, professional development leaders, school administrators, superintendents, board members, and policymakers decide what *not* to do? Turn the page and find the answer. Let us begin the journey of *Transforming Professional Development into Student Results*.

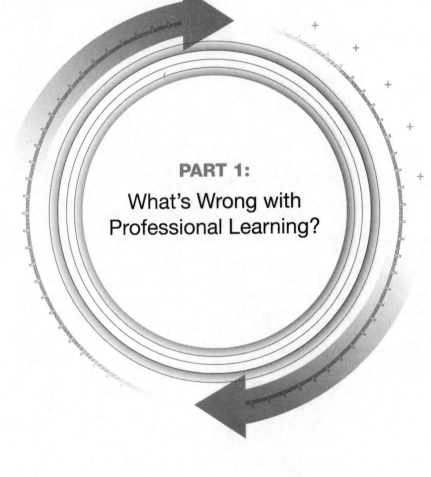

PART 1:

What's Wrong with
Professional Learning?

1

Accountability: Why Autopsies Do Not Improve Patient Health

Imagine that you received the following announcement from your local physician and hospital:

> In a sharp break with tradition, we have decided to start using evidence to make our medical care decisions. We will evaluate carefully the available data and, in the future, engage in more of the practices that improve health and fewer of the practices that appear to kill people.

Would you find this announcement reassuring? Perhaps, on the contrary, you would exclaim, "Isn't that what you have been doing in the past?" The astonishing fact is that evidence-based decision making in medical care is innovative (Pfeffer & Sutton, 2006). Moreover, the most detailed medical evidence on the individual level is the autopsy, a procedure that is undoubtedly filled with data but that rarely improves the health of the patient. There are, of course, exceptions to every rule. In one famous courtroom exchange, the cross-examining attorney asked the medical examiner who had performed an autopsy, "And how did you know that the patient was dead?" The pathologist replied, "Well, his brain and heart had been removed and were in a jar, but I suppose that it's possible that he is out practicing law somewhere."

The Limits of Effect Data

While crime shows captivate television audiences around the globe, viewers would be puzzled by the amiable coroner who announces to the patient, "I've learned what's wrong with you, so just be careful the next time you cross the railroad tracks and you should be fine tomorrow morning." This scenario is no more absurd, however, than the accountability czars who tell schools many months after the end of the school year precisely what was wrong with student achievement. Consider the following typical time line for a process that is euphemistically called school improvement:

- May 15—Students are tested.
- June 30—School improvement plans are due, designed to explain how student achievement in the next year will be better than in the previous year.
- September 1—The superintendent opens the new school year with a declaration that teachers and school leaders must be committed to using data to drive instruction. After the speech, teachers listen to yet another workshop presenter extol the virtues of data, yet no one in the room possesses a single shred of authentic student data that teachers can use to improve teaching practice. "We've got it," they think. "Data good; ignorance bad. Is there anything else before I get back to my classroom to prepare for 35 students tomorrow?"
- October 1—The data that might have informed the June plan or enlightened the September speech at last arrive at schools and classrooms. Unfortunately, teachers are looking at data for students who were in their class the previous year.
- October 2—The local newspaper prints yet another article on the continuing failures of teachers and school leaders.

Some states, no doubt with good intent, have chosen to administer tests in the fall so that they can attempt to provide data to schools in time to influence the current group of students. This policy choice, however well intentioned, has failed. First, test results from the early months of the school year are not a reflection of current curriculum but the outcome of learning attrition over the summer. Second, even these well-intentioned states deliver the data months after the tests, providing data that masquerades as "formative assessment" five or six months into a nine-month school year. Third and most important, the states using fall tests make the dubious claim that they are attempting to provide diagnostic feedback for schools but use the same data to provide evaluative data to the federal government. Thus schools are designated as successes or failures based not on a year's worth of work of teachers and administrators but on six weeks of frantic test preparation.

Assessing the Causes of Learning

Effects are preceded by causes. This statement, obvious in its simplicity, illustrates the central error in current régimes of accountability not only in the world of education but in business as well. As the international economic meltdown that began in 2008 attests, it is entirely possible that organizations with outstanding results can suffer cataclysmic failure when the world is focused only on effects and not on causes. Enron was heralded as one of the most innovative and successful companies in the world in the months before it was insolvent (Neff & Citrin, 1999). Companies that were profiled as successes in such influential books as *Good to Great*—required reading for many leaders in the business, education, and nonprofit sectors—have evaporated (Collins, 2009). We gush with enthusiasm for effects—"Just show me the results!"—but pay little attention to causes. Our attention is diverted to the Scarecrow as he receives his diploma, but we pay no attention to The Man Behind the Curtain.

If this is common sense, then why is it so uncommon? Some states, such as North Carolina, have been remarkably candid about the distance between their aspirations and their accomplishments, and they regularly challenge education leaders to consider the distance between what they claim is important and what they actually do (Reeves, 2009a). The more common practice, however, is the use of blame as a strategy. "The feds made us do it!" cry the states, and school districts and individual schools echo the excuse as they post test scores in charts and graphs that are increasingly colorful and elegant and decreasingly relevant. The practical result of an overemphasis on effect data is reflected in the following conversation:

> *Susan:* I've got it: dropouts are a problem. Ninth grade failure rates are too high, and students who are overage for their grade level and have insufficient credits to graduate with their classmates are most likely to drop out.

> *Ron:* Right. I'm pretty sure we've known that for a long time. So tell me, Susan, how will next year's curriculum, assessment, and intervention policies for our 9th grade students be different than they were last year? Can we do something new today with regard to literacy intervention, student feedback, engagement, and attendance that will improve performance next year?

> *Susan:* It's too late to make any changes.

> *Ron:* But after a student has multiple failures in 9th grade, then we can make some changes?

> *Susan:* Yes. That's the way we have always done it.

> *Ron:* Then why would we expect next year's results to be any better?

> *Susan:* If you're going to be difficult, I'm sending you to a mandatory workshop on 21st century school change.

Patterson, Grenny, Maxfield, McMillan, and Switzler (2008) demonstrated impressively the value of a study of "positive deviance," a powerful research method involving a consideration of cause data next to unexpected effects. An example of positive deviance cited by Patterson and his colleagues involves a study of data related to people suffering from Guinea worm disease. One important value in the study was the observation of how an effect—remarkably less frequent incidence of the disease—could be attributed to causes—behavior differences between the disease-ridden and the relatively disease-free populations despite similar culture, demographics, and economic conditions. Similarly, studies of high-poverty schools that fail are yesterday's news (Coleman et al., 1966), but studies that reveal consistent practices among high-performing, high-poverty schools (Chenoweth, 2007; Reeves, 2004b) consider not only effects but causes. To be sure, a consideration of causes is always a complex matter. Some causes are beyond the control of schools (Rothstein, 2004), whereas other causes are within the sphere of influence of teachers and school leaders (Marzano, 2007; Marzano & Waters, 2009).

This appeal to consider cause data as well as effect data may seem a statement of the obvious. After all, if our objective were to address the teen obesity crisis in North America, we could probably create a more thoughtful program than one consisting of weighing students on May 1 each year, lecturing them in September, and giving them meaningful feedback six months after we last observed them inhaling a bacon cheeseburger. Think for a moment, however, about the extent to which that scenario is any different than knowing—with absolute certainty—in April and May that students need personal intervention and academic assistance but failing to give them any variation in teaching, feedback, or assessment until they experience yet another round of failure and disappointment.

If we expect teachers and school leaders to improve professional practices and decision making, then we must first give them different knowledge and skills than they have received in the past. This common sense, however, is routinely ignored by school leaders and policymakers who validate effects without considering causes.

Consider the case of the high school leader who is absolutely committed to greater equity and opportunity and therefore has undertaken a campaign to increase the number of students who will take college entrance exams. This leader knows that the very act of preparing for and taking those exams—typically the ACT, the SAT, or the A-Levels in Europe—will lead to a process of communication with colleges that will magnify the probability that the student will engage in studies after high school. Students who have traditionally been underrepresented in college will qualify for scholarships; others will receive invitations for interviews and campus visits. As a result, more students will focus on the opportunities and rewards of postsecondary education.

What could possibly go wrong with such a well-intentioned plan? Quite a bit. Compare this school leader with a colleague who is focused intently on effect data—average scores on college entrance exams. The colleague knows that the best way to boost the average is to encourage counselors and teachers to guide only the best-prepared students—perhaps the top 20 to 30 percent—to take those exams. Other students are told in both subtle and direct ways that if they apply to a nonselective college, they need not engage in the expense and demands of the exams. The first leader expands opportunity and equity, while the second leader limits those qualities. Who is the hero?

The newspaper headlines will excoriate the first leader for a disgraceful decline in the average test scores, and the second leader will receive rewards and recognition for another year of rising average scores. There is no adverse consequence for the second leader, who engaged in a systematic effort to diminish opportunity and equity, and there is no positive consequence for the first leader, who sought to do the right thing. In an environment where only effects matter, causes are dismissed as irrelevant. There is a better way, and that is the focus of the remainder of this book.

The Leadership and Learning Matrix

Figure 1.1, The Leadership and Learning Matrix, offers a practical way to consider both effect data and cause data. Student results—typically represented as a percentage of students who are proficient or another appropriate reflection of effect data—are plotted on the vertical axis. The horizontal axis is a representation of the "antecedents of excellence" (Reeves, 2004b; White, 2009), the measurable variables in teaching and leadership that are associated with student achievement.

The upper-left quadrant of the matrix, Lucky, represents schools that have good results and little or no understanding of how those results were achieved. This is not atypical of suburban schools that are host to a daunting number of instructional initiatives and dominated by widely varying teaching strategies. The dizzying array of teaching and leadership styles is defended because the various styles "work"—and evidence of that claim is the invariably high annual test scores. Students in these schools were born into a print-rich environment, were reading before they entered the school system, and when they run into academic trouble, receive healthy doses of parental support and private tutoring. By such logic, physicians are effective in their practice as long as they limit their practice to healthy patients.

FIGURE 1.1
The Leadership and Learning Matrix

	Lucky	**Leading**
Organizational Results	• Good results with no understanding of the reasons • Replication of success not probable	• Good results with clear understanding of the reasons • Replication very probable
	Losing	**Learning**
	• Poor results with no understanding of the reasons • Replication neither probable nor desirable	• Poor results with clear understanding of the reasons • Replication of mistakes not probable

Antecedents of Excellence

The lower-left quadrant, Losing, is the trap waiting for the Lucky schools that have been lulled into complacency. Yesterday's suburban districts are today's urban systems. Parental support and unlimited economic resources are supplanted by families in which two parents work four jobs or, with increasing likelihood, one parent works two or three jobs. Private tutors who created the illusion of success for the Lucky schools have been displaced by a combination of electronic babysitters more intent on destroying the universe than improving math skills. Despite these obvious changes, the Losers witness a decline in results and cling to a deliberate lack of interest in the antecedents of excellence. They return from each "Innovations in Education" conference to see a school with the same schedule, the same teacher assignment policy, and the same feedback system as they have had for decades. They claim to embrace "professional learning communities," but they have merely renamed their faculty meeting. They talk a good game about "assessment for learning" but cling to a regime of final examinations that represents the opposite of that ideal. They have spent enormous sums of financial and political capital to promote "instructional leadership," but leadership time continues to be devoted disproportionately to matters of administration, discipline, and politics. At the highest level of leadership, the time devoted to the care and feeding of board members and other influential politicians far exceeds the time devoted to changing the learning opportunities for students.

The lower-right quadrant, Learning, represents a marked departure from the Losing quadrant. In this quadrant are schools that are taking risks, that are making dramatic changes in leadership, teaching, data analysis, schedule, intervention policies, and feedback systems. Teachers and administrators in these schools are doing everything that their visionary leaders have asked. They take 9th grade students who were reading on a 5th grade level and, with intensive intervention that was decidedly unpopular with students, parents, and many faculty members, moved them to the 8th grade level. Schools in this quadrant include middle schools that required double literacy periods for every single student; students reading at the 3rd grade level moved to the point of almost achieving 6th grade standards, and for the students who were already proficient, the trajectory toward high school success was improved dramatically. Teachers and leaders in these schools improved attendance and discipline and reduced failure rates. They engaged in strategies today that will dramatically reduce the dropout rate next year.

Nevertheless, their results continue to show that most students fail to meet grade-level standards. In the one-column newspaper report on year-end test scores, there appears to be little difference between the Losers and the Learners. In fact, the Losers are portrayed as victims and receive a good deal of sympathy and support from parents and staff members. The Learners, in contrast, endure the worst of both worlds—abused not only for low test scores but also for their attempts to improve student learning. "We worked harder than ever, and what do we have to show for it? Another year of missing Adequate Yearly Progress targets!"

Only the most thoughtful and nuanced school accountability system can differentiate between the Losers and the Learners, yet a growing number of systems have been able to do so. Norfolk Public Schools (Reeves, 2004a, 2006b) won the Broad Prize for Urban Education in 2005 not only because it produced great results, narrowing the achievement gap and improving performance, but also because it documented in a clear and public way the link between causes and effects, between the actions of teachers and school leaders and student results. Their experience is hardly unique (McFadden, 2009), and the preponderance of evidence for three decades has demonstrated that school leadership and teaching influence student results (Goodlad, 1984; Haycock, 1998; Marzano, Waters, & McNulty, 2005; Reeves, 2006b). The Learning quadrant remains the Rodney Dangerfield of education: it "gets no respect" because in a society obsessed with the vertical axis of test scores, the cause data—teacher and leadership actions—remain in analytical oblivion.

The upper-right quadrant, Leading schools, represents the gold standard for education. These are the schools that not only have great student results but also possess a deep understanding of how they achieved those results. But behind every silver lining is a cloud. Today's Leaders could be tomorrow's Lucky or Losing schools. How can such a fall from grace be avoided? The answer is what my colleagues have christened the "5-minute rule," and it applies to almost every sphere of life. If you make a terrible mistake—the examples from this week's news would fill a book, and the same is true of any week in the future in which the reader considers these words—then you should feel awful about it. Engage in abject apology, self-abasement, public humiliation, pillory and post, confession and ... well, we already covered the part about humiliation and apology—for about 4 minutes and 59 seconds. But after 5 minutes, quit the spectacle and get back to work. If, on the other hand, you win an international award for excellence, then call your mom, brag to your friends, and swim in the smug satisfaction of a job well done—but not for more than 4 minutes and 59 seconds. Then get back to work.

Autopsies yield interesting information, but they fail to help the patient. Similarly, educational accountability systems that focus on pathology yield limited information about how to help students whose needs are very much in the present. We must focus not only on effects but also on causes; and in the realm of education, the causes on which we can have the greatest influence are teaching and leadership. In the next chapter, we turn the microscope upside down, focusing not on the students, who are so commonly the object of our inspection, but on teachers and leaders. In particular, we consider the role of professional development strategies on student achievement.

2

Uniform Differentiated Instruction and Other Contradictions in Staff Development

My son and I recently had lunch at a new restaurant in our town. The walls were emblazoned with claims that their french fries were "cholesterol free," a claim that sounded vaguely healthy. I could not avoid noticing, however, that not a single diner in the restaurant was munching solely on the presumably healthy fried potatoes. They accompanied their cholesterol-free side dish with an enormous hamburger, often with bacon, cheese, and fried onions. This is the sort of diet I can easily adopt. The label screams "healthy" while the reality provides full employment for another generation of cardiologists. This chapter considers a similar paradox in the field of education and explores how teachers and leaders can confront the challenges that are required for implementing high-impact professional learning.

High-Impact Professional Learning Defined

High-impact professional learning has three essential characteristics: (1) a focus on student learning, (2) rigorous measurement of adult decisions, and (3) a focus on people and practices, not programs.

First, high-impact professional learning is directly linked to student learning. The most important criterion for evaluating professional learning strategies is not their popularity, ease of adoption, or even the much vaunted imperative for buy-in from stakeholders. (In fact, change at any time is not popular, and therefore any proposed change that garners this mythological level of buy-in is not a meaningful change in professional practice but a label designed to create the illusion of change while scrupulously avoiding the reality of difficult transformation. Professional learning that is devoid of challenge and opposition is the educational equivalent of the double-bacon-cheeseburger diet.) The documentation of the link to student learning occurs at the classroom level, linking specific gains in student learning to specific teaching strategies (Reeves, 2008). Schools cannot claim to be "data driven" when they are guided only by evidence of student learning that reflects no more than a school or district average. That approach is analogous to claiming to want to lose weight but refusing to consider your individual scale reading and relying instead on the average weight of people in your neighborhood or city. High-impact learning is related to student results, and student results must be analyzed one student and one classroom at a time.

The second characteristic of high-impact professional learning is that it balances student results with a rigorous observation of adult practices, not merely a measurement of student results. To continue the health analogy, frequent measurements of weight are strongly associated with successful weight-loss programs (Deutchman, 2007), but weight loss alone is not a sufficient indicator of health. After all, one can lose weight with a combination of amphetamine abuse, depression, and anorexia, but those conditions are rarely associated with improved health. An analysis of our physical health requires a consideration of causes, not merely effects. Similarly, high-impact professional learning is associated with not only a measurement of student learning but also a clear analysis of the decisions of teachers and leaders.

Third, high-impact professional learning focuses on people and practices, not on programs. The past decade of "what works" research (http://

ies.ed.gov/ncee/wwc/) has inadvertently provided a treasure trove of insight on the distinction between people, practices, and programs. After devoting millions of dollars to addressing the question of "what works," the superficial answer based on one report after another showing minimal impact of comprehensive school reform plans is "not much." But a more careful reading of analyses of these studies (Borman, Benson, & Overman, 2009; Gross, Booker, & Goldhaber, 2009) reveals that the brand names of school reform programs are less salient than the depth with which they are implemented. This conclusion is consistent with earlier findings (Reeves, 2008) that claim that the same professional practices were distinguished not by the label ("We're doing professional learning communities" or "We're doing high-yield instructional strategies") but rather by implementation—the extent to which 90 percent or more of teachers were actually using these practices in their classroom.

The greatest frustration for school leaders and classroom educators is the difference between what we know and what we do. We know what effective professional learning looks like. It is intensive and sustained, it is directly relevant to the needs of teachers and students, and it provides opportunities for application, practice, reflection, and reinforcement. We also know what it doesn't look like: death by PowerPoint, ponderous lectures from people who have not been alone with a group of students for decades, and high-decibel whining about the state of (take your pick) children, parents, teachers, public education, and Western civilization.

Many professional development organizations, including the National Staff Development Council (www.nsdc.org), the American Association of School Administrators (www.aasa.org), the National School Boards Association (www.nsba.org), and the publisher of this book, the Association for Supervision and Curriculum Development (www.ascd.org), have established clear frameworks for effective professional learning. It is not the case that we need a new theory of effective professional learning; what we need is a practical mechanism to turn our ideals into reality.

Current Status of Professional Learning

Wei and colleagues (2009) make clear that there is an enormous gap between what teachers expect and what they receive in professional learning. Although more than 90 percent of public school teachers participate in workshops, conferences, and training sessions, "the intensity and duration of most of these learning activities has not deviated far from the traditional one-shot model of professional development" (p. 58). Hayes Mizell (2009a), a Distinguished Senior Fellow at the National Staff Development Council, notes that "most educators have little experience collaborating with their colleagues to determine their learning needs." In his compelling blog (2009b) on professional development, Mizell elaborates:

> Expectations are at the heart of professional development. Many educators don't expect much because they have often been the victims of poorly conceived and executed professional development. Some people responsible for organizing professional development apparently don't expect much either, because they seldom determine whether and to what extent it produces positive results at the classroom level. Even officials who fund professional development don't expect much because they rarely hold anyone accountable for outcomes. Each day, for thousands of educators, this syndrome of low expectations jeopardizes the quality and results of professional development.[1]

We have heard indictments of the "sage on the stage" for decades, but prevailing practices in classroom teaching, teacher evaluation, and professional learning perpetuate rather than diminish this practice. In the classic John Cleese film *A Fish Called Wanda*, the heroine's irrational, unwanted, and homicidal paramour is incensed by any insult to his intelligence. When he is not asking deeply metaphysical questions such as "What would Nietzsche do?" he is dangling the hapless Cleese out the window on a slender rope with the warning, "Don't call me stupid!" While I don't know what

---

[1]Mizell's blog is available at http://www.nsdc.org/learningBlog/archives.cfm/category/hayes-mizell.

Nietzsche would do when confronted with such a gap between research and practice, I am weary of my chosen profession being called stupid. Surely we can't all be irrationally drawn to ineffective policy and practice, can we?

Defending Ineffective Practice

As Cleese might point out after an excruciating interval of avoidance and temporizing, the answer is yes—we can be irrationally drawn to ineffective policy and practice. In fact, we can and do enshrine our ineffectiveness into law. It's a bloody miracle, he might continue, that our irrationality is not engraved in the Constitution.

But wait a moment—it *is* in the Constitution, in the 10th Amendment, part of the Bill of Rights. This is the same hallowed document that protects freedom of religion, speech, and assembly. It protects us from unreasonable search and seizure and grants every citizen the right to a fair trial. And the same document dictates that "the powers not delegated to the United States by the Constitution, nor prohibited by it to the States, are reserved to the States respectively, or to the people." This sentence is the legal foundation of the call for "local control" by state boards of education and school boards across the land. With inexplicable irrationality, the wisdom of James Madison has morphed into the idea that the "reserved powers" clause means that each state (and, in a few cases, each local school board) can vote on whether the square of the hypotenuse is equal to the sum of the squares of the two sides of a right triangle. Matters of science, geography, and reading comprehension are controversies to be adjudicated by elected officials, not matters of fact to be settled based on the available evidence.

Before readers become instantly judgmental about state and local school boards, they should consider an even more dramatic expansion of the abuse of the local control doctrine: site-based decision making. Although the 10th Amendment clearly reserves nonenumerated powers to the states, the new generation of local-control advocates insists that each school, principal, teacher, and parent should identify the curriculum, assessment, and teaching methods it deems most appropriate. Although King George III may have justified rebellion by his abuse of the American Colonies, the subsequent anarchy in Mrs. Carlson's 3rd grade class has been no bargain either. As Marzano and Waters (2009) note, a balance of centralization and local decision making is the most rational approach for school governance.

Defenders of ineffective professional learning, therefore, are neither irrational nor indolent. They are, on the contrary, following a long tradition that elevates local control over common sense. The most striking and disturbing reflection of this sentiment is the recent dissent in the United States Supreme Court in the case of a girl who was strip-searched in pursuit of an over-the-counter pain medication. Although the majority of the Court held that this action was, to put it mildly, an abuse of administrative discretion, the minority claimed that even this egregious and obvious abuse was protected by the nation's historical commitment to local control of schools (Liptak, 2009).

We know what is right not only with regard to prevailing research but also with regard to common sense and personal morality. Yet we persist in tolerating and advocating policies that are unburdened by evidence, opposed by common sense, and in some cases blatantly immoral. One answer might be to stop, think, and reconsider our proliferating initiatives, evaluating each of them carefully against standards of evidence, common sense, and decency. Another answer would be to do more of the same, cramming more initiatives into the limited time available for each teacher and administrator. In the next chapter, we explore why the latter choice has become commonplace in schools.

3

The Law of Initiative Fatigue

Education leaders have three essential resources: time, money, and emotional energy. Time is fixed. Financial resources are typically fixed and, in the present economy, diminishing. Emotional energy is variable but has limits that are exhausted quickly by school leaders who ignore the reality that even the most dedicated employee can be resilient but will refuse to be an eternal Bobo doll, rising from each punch to endure another blow. The Law of Initiative Fatigue states that when the number of initiatives increases while time, resources, and emotional energy are constant, then each new initiative—no matter how well conceived or well intentioned—will receive fewer minutes, dollars, and ounces of emotional energy than its predecessors. This chapter considers the adverse effect of the Law of Initiative Fatigue on high-impact professional learning.

Marie Antoinette and School Reform

"Execution"—for some readers it brings to mind the best-selling book by Larry Bossidy and Ram Charan (2002), a chatty memoir of the joys of corporate leadership before economic reality established that celebrity CEOs and consultants have feet of clay. For other readers, the same term is redolent of earlier centuries in which the guillotine, the auto-da-fé, or the battle axe were all mercifully more brief than management books on the subject of execution. Perhaps the most offensive part of the latest genre in which former business leaders presume to inform the rest of us about effective leadership is their enthusiasm for the "initiative." Even the most infectious enthusiasm for new initiatives is an insufficient condition to create more than 24 hours in a day. Marie Antoinette and Louis XVI lost their heads; those who persist in ignoring the Law of Initiative Fatigue have lost their minds.

The Priority Paradox

White (2005, 2009) establishes with clear and convincing evidence that there is an inverse relationship between the number of priorities that leaders pursue and their long-term effectiveness. Technology sometimes encourages people to confuse busyness with effectiveness. The extremely important leader, the myth goes, handles an increasingly large number of priorities, rushing from one place to another, handling a couple of cell phone conversations while texting and e-mailing others—all while driving or sitting in a meeting. Perhaps these people think they are being efficient and effective, but recent research punctures this myth. Multitasking is more accurately described as "switch-tasking" (Crenshaw, 2008). When we are interrupted, on average, every two or three minutes, a task that could be completed in half an hour will remain uncompleted for day after day. When we fail to focus, concentrate, and deliberately eliminate distractions and interruptions, then the cost to individual and organizational effectiveness is extraordinary (Gallagher, 2009; Pennebaker, 2009). If you believe that you are focused, consider the following question: In the past 30 minutes, how many of the following things have you done?

_____ Talk on the telephone
_____ Listen to voicemail
_____ Read e-mail
_____ Text message

_____ Instant message

_____ Hold a personal conversation

_____ Read this book

_____ Glance at a newspaper or magazine article near you

_____ Write e-mail

_____ Make a note in your "to-do" list

_____ Respond to a fire drill (some interruptions are unavoidable)

_____ Get your child/spouse/colleague some milk/vodka/coffee

Please enter all the interruptions I've failed to think of here:

_____

_____

If you checked six or more items, then you are a card-carrying member of the ADHD (Adults Disoriented by Hyperbolic Demands) club. If you checked between two and five, then you are stressed, unfocused, and a bit upset that anyone is pointing out that you are less than perfect. If you checked one or two, then either you are not reading very carefully or I owe you a deep apology for interrupting your Zen-like meditative state.

Power Standards for Teachers and Leaders

The concept of "power standards" (Ainsworth, 2003a) is a response to the simple truth that there are too many academic content standards for teachers and not enough time in the typical academic year in which to teach those standards. The criteria for power standards (Reeves, 2004b) include the following:

• **Leverage**—Standards that influence more than a single discipline. Examples include nonfiction writing skills that help students in reading comprehension, mathematics, science, social studies, and every other pursuit; tables, charts, and graphs—useful in science, social studies, math, and language arts; and critical-thinking and problem-solving skills that transcend every discipline. For teachers and school leaders, the principle of leverage includes such concepts as feedback and engagement, standards of professional learning that are appropriate to every discipline and grade level.

- **Endurance**—Standards that will have relevance longer than the time it takes to administer a single test. Number sense is as important for algebra students as it is for 2nd graders; comprehension of a main idea and supporting details is useful for both the high school senior and the kindergartner struggling to read.

- **Essential for the Next Level**—As a teacher and teacher of teachers, I know that I'm much better at giving advice than taking it. If you ask me, "What are you willing to give up?" with regard to the curriculum for my students this year, I will readily reply, "Nothing—everything I do is important!" But if you ask, "What advice will you give to the teacher in the next-lower grade with respect to the knowledge and skills that students need in order to enter your class next year with confidence and success?" then I can provide a list that is succinct and focused. Figure 3.1, for example, provides a list of power standards for middle school students.

Surely the list of standards in Figure 3.1 omits dozens of typical middle school academic standards. Nevertheless, I challenge each reader to ask a high school teacher the following questions:

- If students entering your class are able to meet these standards, will they have a high probability of success, even if their middle school marks are low?
- If students entering your class are not able to meet these standards, will they have any chance of success, even if their middle school marks merit the honor roll?

It is clear that we are able to articulate standards for students. Why, then, should we not be able to establish standards for adult learning? If we are to avoid the effect of the Law of Initiative Fatigue, then we must first prioritize the learning standards that teachers and administrators will

FIGURE 3.1
Suggested Power Standards for Middle School Students

Writing, Reading, and Social Studies

Students will use Standard English, including proper grammar, spelling, and punctuation, to complete the following independently evaluated essays. Teachers will evaluate the essays using the same districtwide writing rubric that is routinely used in the classroom for all writing assignments.

- *Narrative*: Given a new short story of approximately 1,500 words, students will write a five-paragraph essay describing the setting, characters, and plot.
- *Analytical*: Write a five-paragraph essay comparing the points of view expressed in two authentic historical documents.
- *Persuasive*: Write a letter to the editor of a local newspaper expressing a point of view on a topic of interest. Include evidence to support your point of view.

Mathematics and Science

- Perform number operations (addition, subtraction, multiplication, and division) from ten-thousandths to millions with and without a calculator.
- Given a story problem presented in narrative form, draw a picture that describes the problem and write word and number sentences that describe the steps to the solution.
- Draw an accurate two-dimensional scale drawing of a real-world object. Include a demonstration of an understanding of the properties of rectangles and triangles, complete linear and area measurements, and accurate use of scale.
- Given a scientific question, generate a hypothesis, design an experiment, conduct measurements of at least two variables, place the data in a table, create an appropriate graph from the data in the table, and write a paragraph that correctly states the conclusions to be drawn from the experiment.

Teamwork, Organization, and Service

Participate in a team in which each student shares responsibility for planning, organization, and execution of an original idea with value to fellow students and school community. Submit the project to evaluation by teachers and other adults.

Source: Adapted from "The Power Standards: What Middle School Students Need to Enter High School with Confidence and Success," by The Leadership and Learning Center. Copyright © 2009 by The Leadership and Learning Center. Adapted with permission.

find most essential to be effective in their professional responsibilities. For example, every teacher must do the following:

- Understand academic content in the current grade level and the next grade level.
- Provide feedback to students in a timely, accurate, and effective manner.
- Prepare lessons that are engaging, adaptive, and differentiated.
- Demonstrate an understanding of the individual needs of each student.

Every school administrator must do the following:

- Understand the academic requirements of a particular school in relation to the schools that send students to, and receive students from, the administrator's school.
- Provide feedback to teachers and other staff members in a timely, accurate, and effective manner.
- Prepare staff meetings and professional development opportunities that are engaging, adaptive, and differentiated.
- Demonstrate an understanding of the individual needs of each staff member.

A pattern appears to be emerging, and the reader can fill in the blanks for the requirements for educational leaders at the district, state, and national levels. The clear imperative for educational leadership is *focus*. Unfortunately, the typical response of leaders at every level is diffusion, often in the guise of strategic plans. In the next chapter, we explore the potential strengths and limitations of school plans and challenge the myths that pervade this black hole of resources, time, and energy.

4

The Myths and Realities of Planning

Initiative fatigue does not occur by either accident or malice. Teachers and school leaders do not deliberately overload their task lists with more items than they can conceivably accomplish. Neither do state, provincial, or national policymakers intend the inevitable results of the Law of Initiative Fatigue that were explored in Chapter 3. Each document request has a well-intended purpose, and each element of a required plan is a response to a perceived need. Nevertheless, despite overwhelming evidence that limited time is a source of dissatisfaction among teachers (Ingersoll & Perda, 2009), the burdens associated with mandatory planning documents are proliferating at an alarming rate. This chapter considers the reasoning behind the planning requirements and suggests constructive alternatives for school and system leaders and policymakers.

Testing the Planning Hypothesis

The idea that planning is associated with results is long established in the leadership literature for business, nonprofit, and educational organizations (Bernhardt, 2004; Kaplan & Norton, 1996, 2000; Kaufman, 1995). The adage "If you fail to plan, then you are planning to fail" seems to make sense. Plans, from daily task lists to master plans for complex projects, bring order to what might otherwise be chaos. Nevertheless, the question remains: If required school improvement plans have grown in number and size over the years, why has there not been a corresponding improvement in student results? Schmoker (2004) launched a national controversy when he labeled many planning models as "feckless reform" and observed that they were "hugely popular, but patently discredited" (p. 424). Joyce (2004) and Cook (2004) responded in separate articles with partial agreement and complete disagreement, respectively. The debate, however, should be reframed to move away from the extremes of centralized planning versus effective reform to a more narrowly focused question: Which specific characteristics of educational plans are most related to student achievement?

What my colleagues and I at The Leadership and Learning Center found in the course of our research on school planning, implementation, and monitoring is nothing less than astonishing. When examining student achievement gains and losses by students in the schools for which we examined more than 2,500 improvement plans, an interesting pattern emerged. It is not the case that planning is always successful or always unsuccessful. Rather, plans have specific characteristics that have a direct, consistent, positive, and powerful relationship to student results. Certain other planning practices are unrelated or only weakly related to student results. And a few planning practices, unfortunately, are inversely related to student results. These findings are not likely to satisfy either extreme in the planning debate, but the task of this chapter is to present the evidence and let the reader decide the case on the merits. For readers who desire a more detailed look at the statistical evidence, a complete set of charts that describe the data in this chapter and the rest of the book is contained in Appendix A. The detailed definitions of each variable in the study are listed in Appendix B.

Plans Associated with Success

In general, the study found that plans with the following nine characteristics had a measurable and significant effect on gains in student achievement in reading and mathematics in elementary, middle, and high school:

- **Comprehensive Needs Assessment**—The plans contained evidence of school leadership decisions regarding the use of time, assignment of staff, and allocation of resources that were directly related to student needs.
- **Inquiry Process**—The plans identified causal relationships between teaching and leadership practices and student results.
- **Prioritization**—The plans had six or fewer clearly established priorities.
- **Specificity**—The plan goals were directly related to academic expectations for students, including specific focus on grade levels, skills, and individual students.
- **Measurability**—The learning community could make an objective statement about the progress or lack of it in their school with regard to the achievement of goals.
- **Achievability**—The goals were sufficiently challenging to close learning gaps within three to five years.
- **Relevance**—The goals represented urgent, critical needs and were clearly aligned with the needs-analysis process.
- **Timeliness**—The goals had specific dates—season, month, or day—for assessment, data collection, and analysis.
- **Monitoring**—The plans included specific data to be monitored, along with frequent intervals for examining and reporting progress. Monitoring included not only student results but also professional practices of teachers and school leaders.

The gains varied from one grade level to the next and between math and science, but the overall trend was consistent. When leaders took these characteristics seriously and implemented them in a way that resulted in the highest score on a three-level scoring rubric, then student achievement gains were significantly greater than when they scored at the lowest level. In a separate analysis of a subset of 330 of the 2,500 schools in the study, Fernandez (2006) found that schools with the greatest increases in these same characteristics also had the greatest gains in achievement. Moreover, he concluded that the effect was greatest for high-poverty, low-performing schools.

The Nonlinear Model of Planning

Readers have learned, however, to beware of undifferentiated checklists. We are interested in not only the relationship between general planning characteristics and student achievement but also the nuances behind the data. If this research has a consistent finding that will be useful to educators, school leaders, and policymakers, it is this: the relationship of leadership decision making in school planning to student achievement is *nonlinear.*

In other words, it is simply not true that as a school progresses from quality levels 1 to 2 and then to 3, it should expect comparable student gains at each level. In some cases, the results *are* neatly linear. For example, a review of the relationship between grade 8 reading results and timely goals (see Appendix A, Figure A.1) showed 4 percent gains for schools scoring a 1 (that is, fewer than half the goals were associated with any sort of time requirement); 27.2 percent gains for level 2 (that is, the majority of goals were associated with a time requirement); and 43.7 percent gains for level 3 (that is, all of the school goals were associated with a time require-ment). But other relationships were more perplexing, showing little differ-ence between levels 1 and 2, or even a decline from level 1 to level 2. That disconcerting condition was true with regard to grade 4 reading and the measurability of goals (see Appendix A, Figure A.15) and grade 5 reading and research-based strategies (see Appendix A, Figure A.19). In other words, half-hearted implementation was actually worse than minimal or no implementation.

The nonlinear finding of this research is of critical importance for school leaders who are planning professional learning. An extraordinary amount of energy, time, and money is invested in low-level work—exposure to general ideas—and the initial stages of implementation. Change then often stalls as leaders fail to follow through in their efforts or as teachers are frustrated by the ineffectiveness of the early stages of change. Yet the evidence suggests that deep implementation is essential for an effect on student results.

This conclusion is directly consistent with the findings of an earlier study (Reeves, 2006b) that evaluated 15 different claims for initiatives within schools, ranging from professional learning communities to collaborative scoring to nonfiction writing programs. Although each of the more than 200 schools in the study made nearly identical claims regarding implementation, further inquiry revealed that actual implementation of those initiatives by classroom teachers ranged from less than 10 percent to more than 90 percent. An examination of their reading, math, and science scores revealed that schools with more than 90 percent implementation experienced achievement gains that were three to five times higher than schools with the identical professional learning claims but less than 10 percent implementation.

Sharratt and Fullan (2009) concluded that effective districtwide reform depends upon deep interdependent practice—the opposite of the promulgation of plans and policies without collaboration or sustainability. Marzano and colleagues (2005) similarly concluded that focus was an essential component for school-level leadership, and Marzano and Waters (2009) echoed that finding for district-level leaders. It is particularly noteworthy that three sets of researchers operating independently and using different analytical techniques—case studies (Sharratt & Fullan, 2009), meta-analysis (Marzano et al., 2005), and quantitative analysis (the present study)—came to two remarkably similar conclusions. First, leadership decisions have a decisive effect on student results. Second, the effect of leadership is not the result of a neat linear progression; but rather, deep implementation and clear focus on a few critical factors are essential. The nonlinear model of implementation impact is illustrated in Figure 4.1.

Getting School and System Planning Right

The practical implication of this model is that school leaders must make the difficult choice to move from superficial compliance with a myriad of directives for school plans toward selective and deep implementation of a few areas of focus. The challenge to policymakers is a dramatic reconsideration

FIGURE 4.1
Nonlinear Model of Implementation

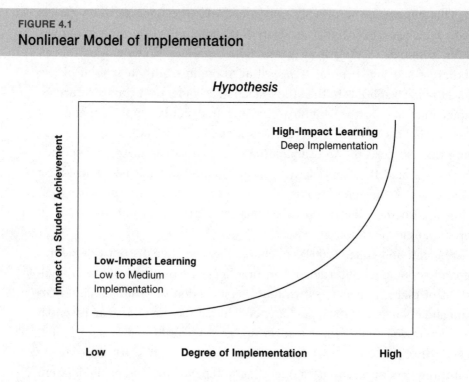

Hypothesis

High-Impact Learning
Deep Implementation

Low-Impact Learning
Low to Medium
Implementation

Impact on Student Achievement

Low   **Degree of Implementation**   High

All Results

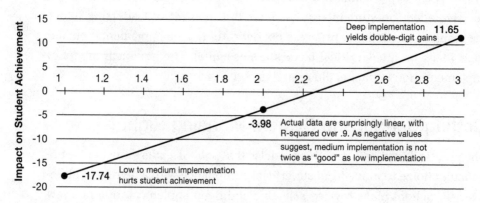

Deep implementation **11.65**
yields double-digit gains

-3.98   Actual data are surprisingly linear, with
R-squared over .9. As negative values
suggest, medium implementation is not
twice as "good" as low implementation

-17.74 Low to medium implementation
hurts student achievement

Degree of Implementation

Positive Results Only

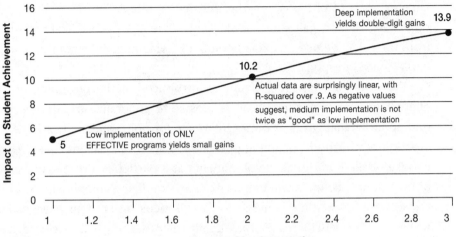

Negative Results Only

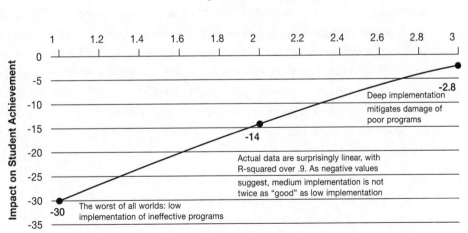

of the format, content, and quantity of requirements for school plans. If the intent of educational policies is to improve student achievement, then the evidence suggests that this purpose is not served by the mere presence or absence of plans, whether labeled "strategic," "improvement," or otherwise. Rather, gains in student achievement are most likely to result from the selective use of a small number of planning elements that can be implemented deeply.

Even the nine planning elements introduced at the beginning of this chapter can be misleading, as it is unwise to generalize from large-scale data to individual cases. A better inference for policymakers would be the creation of a menu of planning options and the requirement that schools choose—based on the needs of students at a particular time—a few areas of focus. Some schools will emphasize parental involvement, whereas others will pursue writing; some schools will focus on student engagement, whereas others will increase dramatically their teaching of and feedback for reading. Large-scale improvement is most likely to occur when a few school improvement initiatives are implemented deeply, not when a laundry list of initiatives is implemented in a scattershot manner.

Although the evidence in favor of focus is significant, the prevailing trends appear to be taking schools in precisely the opposite direction. Initiative fatigue is bad enough; program proliferation is even worse, as it creates a dependency by schools on brand names rather than professional practices. In the next chapter, we explore the fallacy behind a reliance on brand names. This is not an argument against publishers who reasonably seek to protect their intellectual property. Rather, this analysis suggests that effective implementation of any educational reform is not dependent upon labels or brands, but upon deep changes in professional practices and leadership decisions.

5

Mr. McGuffey Doesn't Teach Here:
The Brand-Name Fallacy

William Holmes McGuffey could scarcely have imagined that more than 120 million of his books would influence generations of students. *McGuffey's Readers* served for more than a century as a staple of elementary education in the United States. Originated in 1836 and most recently revised in 1879, the *Readers* can seem jarring to the 21st century reader. The language is complex, and the overt patriotic and religious messages depart from the decidedly neutral tone that contemporary textbook publishers have adopted in order to survive a competitive selection process. Nevertheless, the *Readers* serve to illustrate an important point, particularly as they are now undergoing a resurgence of popularity in some quarters. Consider an excerpt from the *Fourth Reader* (McGuffey, 1879/1997). In the Kentucky and Ohio towns from which McGuffey wrote, few students would graduate from high school, and only the wealthy elite would attend college. Still, the vast majority of students in the 19th century would make it through 4th grade, where they would encounter passages such as this one:

> The eagle seems to enjoy a kind of supremacy over the rest of the inhabit-
> ants of the air. Such is the loftiness of his flight, that he often soars in the
> sky beyond the reach of the naked eye, and such is his strength that he

has been known to carry away children in his talons. But many of the noble
qualities imputed to him are rather fanciful than true. (p. 84)

The passage continues with details that are dramatic and so engaging that
they would lure the most uninterested reader into a trance as surely as
Harry Potter, Redwall, and other series of the modern era. In all three cases,
the authors engage young readers by employing complex language and
challenging content in a manner that conveys deep respect for 10-year-old
readers. Reading experts can quarrel about the grade level of McGuffey's
passage, one that is certainly not the most complex in the book. The most
casual observer, however, could compare the passage to a 4th grade reader
of today and notice that the former is significantly more complex in vocabu-
lary and style. The Flesch-Kinkaid grade level for the McGuffey passage
is 9.4, and a review of four other popular reading-level estimates yields a
mean score of 9.48. (Readers can perform their own readability and grade-
level analyses of text for free at http://www.addedbytes.com/readability.)
We can draw two potential inferences from this illustration. The first is
the lament that the present-day publishers of the *Readers* hope consumers
will express: according to a consensus of five different estimates of grade
levels for text readability, a 21st century student would require twice as
many years of schooling as would a 19th century student to grasp the same
text. Bring back McGuffey in order to save the morality, patriotism, and
reading abilities of our children! An alternative inference is that, as splendid
a fellow and sincere a Calvinist as Mr. McGuffey may have been, he does not
own the alphabet any more than Bill Gates owns the Internet. If our heart's
desire is to provide students with more challenging and engaging reading,
then we need teachers and parents who are willing to do what William
McGuffey, J. K. Rowling, and Brian Jacques did—trust that if the reading
material is sufficiently engaging, young readers can be counted upon to
struggle with the material and not only will rise to the challenge but will
enjoy it. It is not, in brief, the McGuffey brand name that creates fascination
with reading, but the practices and people in the classroom who do so.

Programs, Practices, or People?

Call it the "McGuffey dilemma." Should schools invest in programs, or should they instead focus on practices and people? Calegari (Colin, 2009) provides the unequivocal response:

> The single most important change we need is to elevate the status of public school teachers and transform the profession into one that is truly prestigious, wildly competitive, and financially attractive. Until we get and keep the smartest teachers in the classrooms, I fear that none of these other reforms, no matter how well designed, will truly achieve what we so desperately need for our schools and kids.

Fuhrman and Elmore (2004) have argued that the consequences for failure now fall on students, but

> stakes for educators are highly diffused throughout the organizational structures in which they work, so it is relatively easy for accountability systems, in the absence of countervailing pressures, to ratchet up stakes on students—the unrepresented constituency—and to allow stakes for institutions and educators to become increasingly diffuse. (p. 292)

Ask a dozen educators to evaluate the most popular programs and an argument will quickly ensue. "It was great!" exclaims the first teacher, noting improvements in student achievement and engagement. "It was worthless!" counters the second, explaining failures in technology, training, leadership support, and available time. Advocates of the program in question will insist that if results are inconsistent, it is because the administrators and teachers involved failed to exhibit adequate fidelity to the reform model. Critics will argue that the flaws of the program itself were to blame. This exchange of blame is, however, not particularly illuminating if we are to address the basic conflict among programs, practices, and people. Assuming for the sake of argument that "fidelity to the model" is the key to research-based programs, it is a living, breathing teacher, not R2-D2 ("Right away, Master Luke!") or, depending on one's generational perspective, HAL ("I'm afraid I can't let you do that, Dave"), who will actually implement any instructional model in the classroom.

In an economic environment in which educational funding is wildly inconsistent from one jurisdiction to the next and from one year to the next, today's programs invariably have the potential to be tomorrow's dinosaurs. Perhaps they will produce something of value, like oil, but it may take a few million years. People and practices endure; programs rarely do. Consider this simple experiment. List all of the new instructional program initiatives of the past five years that you recall. Compare that list to those that will be in place and actively monitored next year. The gap between yesterday's good intentions and tomorrow's reality will be filled in one of two ways. First, yet another program will replace the previous pony on the merry-go-round, a presumption that depends upon unpredictable funding. The second and more likely scenario is that the gap will be filled by the daily decisions of educators and school administrators. When the software licenses expire, the three-ring binders are lost, and the training is long forgotten, teachers will continue to have students walk into the classroom. Administrators will continue to work with teachers who need support and encouragement. In these many moments of truth, it will be people and the professional practices they carry with them, not brand names, that define success or failure.

Implementation Essentials

The research detailed in Appendix A, along with a combination of previous quantitative analyses, qualitative studies, and meta-analyses, suggests that when it comes to implementation of instructional interventions, a few specific decisions of school leaders have a disproportionate effect on student learning. Three clear priorities include teacher assignment, monitoring practices, and time allocation. In logical terms, these are "necessary but not sufficient" conditions for success. Although these conditions alone may not ensure student success, school leaders who attempt to create an environment for improvement without accounting for the primacy of teacher quality, providing effective feedback and monitoring, or creating sufficient time for implementation will have almost no chance of success, no matter how earnestly a new program is implemented.

Yun and Moreno (2006) provide evidence of the disproportionate way in which teacher quality is allocated among schools based on the ethnicity and economic status of students. Haycock (1998) documented the clear and consistent relationship between teacher quality and student results. Nevertheless, the prevailing tradition, often codified in collective bargaining agreements and established practice, is that teachers with the most experience and seniority can choose to remove themselves from the vicinity of students who need them the most. The good news is that when these traditions are challenged, great things happen. Case studies in which senior teachers formerly assigned to advanced placement classes take on the most challenging students in a school (Reeves, 2009b) confirm that the most immediate results for student achievement happen when the most effective teachers are provided to the students with the greatest needs.

The monitoring practices of school and system leaders tend to be the educational equivalent of autopsies. The results may be interesting, but they are too late to provide much benefit to the patient. Previous research on monitoring practices (Reeves, 2006b) suggests that leaders must provide monitoring that focuses on adult actions (not merely on student test scores), that is frequent, and that is constructive. Just as Marzano (2007) found that the frequency of feedback from teachers to students is directly related to gains in student performance, so Colvin (2008) has more recently documented that adults who aspire to professional levels of expertise require frequent observation, coaching, and feedback in order to make substantive improvement.

The third necessary (if not sufficient) condition for successful deep implementation of professional learning initiatives is time. Although providing additional class time and collaboration time for teachers is alone not sufficient to ensure improved student results, the failure of leaders to provide sufficient time is almost certainly fatal to reform efforts. At the very least, leaders can examine critically the absurd ways in which time is routinely misallocated in schools. Here are a few examples:

- **Pull-outs**—Students are removed from a literacy class to get "extra" literacy. Putting aside the obvious—that perfect execution of this plan does not result in additional time for student literacy—the practical result is that every transition takes time, perhaps 5 minutes at the beginning and end of the pull-out, or about 50 minutes per week. Therefore, during a 36-week school year, students who are victims of these pull-out programs actually receive 30 fewer hours of literacy instruction than students who did not need this intervention.

- **Announcements**—This odd tradition is continued by administrators afflicted with the "microphone fantasy," the irrational belief that the person in possession of the microphone on a public address system is also in possession of the attention of students and adults in a school. A small number of schools are experimenting with alternative ways of conveying information to students and faculty members, and a few bold ones are willing to abolish them completely with the sole exception of emergency communications. Faculty and department meetings can potentially offer an environment for professional learning, but not if the first third of a meeting is consumed by oral announcements that could have been made in writing.

- **E-mail**—Although this is an undeniably fast method of communication, it is also undifferentiated, forcing real priorities to compete with pharmaceutical ads, with each "ping" announcing another deposit in the mailbox. There is at least a hint of hypocrisy in the air when adults routinely confiscate the cell phones of students and, after delivering another lecture on the virtues of following the rules and paying attention, they can be found responding to e-mail during meetings, professional learning, and even during class.

The list of ways that time is consumed unwisely is a long one, and a profitable way for educators and administrators to begin every semester is to take an inventory of their best time-saving ideas. Transitions can be hastened, schedules can be made more rational, and e-mail can be turned off (try it, just for three hours, and see what happens to your level of focus and concentration, once you get over the nasty withdrawal symptoms).

Fragmentation and lack of focus are not merely symptoms of a medical condition commonly associated with hyperactive boys. Institutional attention deficits are self-inflicted. We know that the effectiveness of multitasking is a myth for students—they are not *both* writing their English essay *and* sending text messages to their friends, but merely switching back and forth between the two (or many more) tasks. That they perform these multiple feats quickly and enthusiastically does not make them effective. Institutional multitasking is no more effective, as we shall see in the next chapter.

6

Scattershot Learning: "If It's Tuesday, It Must Be Brain Research"

The contradictions of many professional learning practices are deeply ingrained in traditions. Early in teacher education programs, we require that candidates for our profession take examinations and write research papers on the virtues of cooperative learning—entirely alone. To do otherwise might compromise a university honor code. We lecture leaders about the importance of distributed leadership, often at conferences to which only senior leaders have been invited. Early in my career, I would exhort seminar participants on the virtues of formative assessment—and then read the feedback they provided to me after the seminar was complete, too late to inform my teaching.

Much older and only a little wiser, I now ask seminar participants during the first five minutes of our work together to complete the following sentence: "Today will be a success if _____." Please take a moment and complete that sentence for yourself. Think of your next professional learning experience, and consider what would make it worth your time and energy. That day will be a success if _____.

With certainty that is rare in educational research, I can predict that the response of the vast majority of readers will be "If I could just get one or two ideas that I can apply in the classroom when I return to school." That's it? Just one or two ideas as a result of six or more hours of labor? This is, by far, the most common response that I receive, and it is a reflection of our generally low expectations for professional learning.

The state of professional learning is not quite as bad as all that—it's worse. Rather than provide the one or two useful ideas for which our colleagues are pleading, some programs are actively counterproductive, crowding out useful practices with useless and time-consuming programs. The problem is particularly acute for schools that face the greatest challenges in student learning. Hayes Mizell (2009b) wrote:

> We all know that teachers in low-performing schools are under tremendous pressures to increase their students' learning. But simply telling them they have to "improve" usually has little effect. Providing more money for new academic intervention programs may at best produce only marginal increases in student achievement. Cascading, multiple remedies intended to fix a school frequently confuse teachers, causing them to lose focus and further dissipate their limited time and energy.... No Child Left Behind requires that schools in "improvement status" must use 10 percent of their Title I funds for "high-quality professional development" that directly addresses "the academic achievement problem that caused the school to be identified for school improvement." But the law does not acknowledge or address the possibility of a *professional development problem* that may have actually *contributed* to the school falling into improvement status in the first place.... In many low-performing schools, there is not only too little professional learning, but too much of it is ineffective. Professional development cannot be part of the solution unless it is no longer part of the problem.

When Professional Learning Is the Problem

The failure of school systems to focus in their professional learning endeavors is in many respects a self-inflicted wound. Although certainly a good deal of blame must be placed on the shoulders of professional developers, it is to the great credit of leading professional development organizations that they have recognized and challenged this problem. At the same time, membership organizations are driven by the demands of their members, and those demands are invariably for the newest, latest, and greatest ideas. "We had that last year" is the kiss of death for proposed professional learning activities. Consider the aspiring professional athlete who tells her coach, "I had those exercises last year—I'm only interested in something new!" Coyle (2009) and Colvin (2008), in two remarkably insightful books on the development of human talent, concur that one of the greatest inhibitions to the development of human potential is the aversion to effective practice. Although a generation of teachers has been led to believe that "drill and kill" is a terrible idea, the truth is that skills for students and adults develop with deliberate practice. The *Cambridge Handbook of Expertise and Expert Performance* (Ericsson, Charness, Feltovich, & Hoffman, 2006) is an exhaustive review of the research on the subject, and the book's inescapable conclusion is that whether the subject is baseball or biology, piano or paleontology, medicine or math, children and adults need deliberate practice in order to achieve their objectives.

My research (Reeves, 2004a, 2006a) has applied this principle to the work of educators and school leaders. Consider, for example, the skills necessary for collaborative scoring. After years—decades in many cases—of evaluating student work against our own idiosyncratic criteria, it is a challenge to reach consensus with one's colleagues. They are too easy or too hard, too ambiguous or too literal, too sensitive to the needs of individual students or too indifferent to the need for objectivity. When working with a group of college-educated and deeply sincere professionals who want only the best for the children they serve, I found an astonishingly low level of consensus among them about what constituted proficient student work. Collaboration, it turns out, is not a gift from the gods but a skill that requires effort and practice. This is precisely the conclusion that drove the Cambridge researchers and inspired Coyle and Colvin. Ainsworth (2003b) found the same phenomenon with regard to the work of teachers and administrators in improving assessments. Years of practice on the same area of focus in their professional learning—the creation of engaging classroom assessments based on clear academic content standards— yielded vastly superior professional work and student results.

When people young and old focus, they improve performance. When they are diffuse in their energy, they stagnate. Handel's eighth oratorio was better than his first; Beethoven's ninth symphony was better than his first; Curie's tenth experiment was more insightful than her first. Venus Williams's one thousandth serve was better than her first. Consider what might have happened if any of these people had said, "I don't want to work on this—I did it last year."

Perhaps the most pithy synthesis of the research on developing expertise by students and teachers was expressed by Howard (2009): smart is not something you are; smart is something you get. If we expect the educational professions to "get smart," then we must be willing to focus. That means that we abandon our appetite for the new and pursue instead the disciplines related to expertise. Those disciplines include focus, repetition, and effective practice. Because time for professional learning is limited, this means that we make explicit choices to exclude rather than embrace the latest, greatest, and newest ideas. To this end, there are two essential questions every educational leader must address:

• If I require every teacher and administrator to "get trained" in my latest enthusiasm, what great ideas of last year am I willing to displace?

• Are the children in our schools better served by teachers and administrators who have deep insight and knowledge of last year's skills, or superficial exposure to this year's fads?

From Frantic to Focused

The dilemma suggested by these two essential questions is solved by our wise counselor Mizell (2009c), who has proposed a new taxonomy of professional development:

1. Preservice education
2. Courses for recertification

3. Training

4. Information dissemination

5. Presentations

6. Powerful designs

With regard to "powerful designs"—the top of the taxonomy—Easton (2008) suggests that there are 20 strategies that can do better than, as Mizell gently suggests, merely engaging the "rears and ears" of participants. Unfortunately, a great deal of professional learning is stuck in level 3 of the taxonomy, "training," with the exasperating use of the passive voice. The phrase "our teachers were trained" is nearly as offensive and ineffective as saying "my pit bulls were trained" when the canines sink their teeth into your calves. Mammals (and many other life forms) learn, and only rarely are they trained.

Assessing Your Professional Learning

Is your school system frantic or focused? Here are some questions you may wish to consider. It's not a test and there is no score. Rather, these questions are designed to solicit genuine conversation about the future direction of your professional learning:

• Find a professional learning presentation, seminar, or institute that you had 36 months ago. Stop, check the calendar, and find one that is at least three years old. What do you remember about it?

• Can you name one or two specific influences that this program had on your teaching and leadership practice today?

• As you reviewed the calendar of previous professional development programs, to what extent were you surprised by the recollection of programs and ideas that seemed inspiring at the time but are today no longer relevant?

• Consider your professional development calendar for the year ahead—look at a full 12 months from the date you are reading this. What proportion of the available dates are blank—yet to be completed based on an unknown topic or a speaker whose availability is not yet determined?

• What proportion of your professional learning calendar for the year ahead suggests a commitment to the refinement, reinforcement, and deliberate practice and perfection of the professional practices that you know are most essential for your schools?

This chapter concludes our consideration of what is wrong with professional learning. We now leave this difficult but necessary self-examination and turn toward the productive territory of how professional learning can become engaging, insightful, and productive. In the next chapter, we consider the seismic shift from vision to implementation. Institutional multitasking is no more effective than individual multitasking, as we shall see in the next chapter. Compelling evidence suggests that teachers, school leaders, and students are much better served when professional learning is focused on the deep and consistent implementation of a few things. That is, however, contrary to the general trend of professional learning that is characterized by the introduction of many ideas but the deep implementation of few if any of them. Just as fragmented efforts are ineffective at the individual level, an organization's failure to focus inhibits learning for both adults and students.

PART 2:

How to Create High-Impact Professional Learning

7

From Vision to Implementation

If gold represents the vision, platinum represents the implementation. The "golden rule" in several different belief systems that have survived for thousands of years typically enjoins us to do to others what we would have them do to us. The "platinum rule" (Reeves & Allison, 2009) suggests that we should do *better* for others than we would expect them to do for us. Although many leadership theories espouse the virtues of shared vision, the thesis of this chapter is that vision without implementation is counterproductive. It not only fails to achieve the intended objectives but also engenders cynicism and distrust.

From Intention to Evidence

One of the most important transitions in education in the past decade has been the embrace of academic standards as the prevailing method for evaluation of students. This is a seismic shift from the presumption of the past that the primary function of schools was to compare students to one another rather than to an objective standard.

This important transformation has four essential implications for every teacher, administrator, and policymaker. First, tests scores alone are not a sufficient reflection of student learning, but we must base our conclusions on the evidence of student success. Wiggins and McTighe (2005) suggest that students must explain, interpret, apply, have perspective, have empathy for the views of others, and possess self-knowledge of their own understandings. Their evidentiary bar is far higher than a claim of proficiency based on a test score or the smug satisfaction gained by beating a fellow student in a race against the clock. Second, the fundamental purpose of assessment is not merely to evaluate students but to teach them. Stiggins (2007) thoughtfully distinguishes between assessment *of* learning and assessment *for* learning. Third, assessment is most effective as a preventive rather than a remediating or punitive strategy. Wiliam (2007) suggests the use of a preflight checklist for students before they submit assignments to teachers. As a former pilot, I find Wiliam's metaphor compelling, as the checklists completed on the ground are decidedly less stressful than those conducted in the air. For example, part of every preflight checklist for almost every aircraft is a physical inspection of pitot tubes, devices that provide essential information to the pilots about airspeed. It is impossible to conduct this test in the air. By the time the pilot learns that the pitot tubes are clogged, it may be too late to remedy the situation. Fourth, the purpose of assessment in a standards-based environment is not only to provide feedback to students for improvement but also to improve the performance of teachers and leaders (Ainsworth & Viegut, 2006).

How would our approach to professional learning be different if we applied these four standards not only to the assessment of student learning but also to the actions of teachers and administrators? First, we wouldn't use a test score as evidence of proficiency for a teaching professional any more than we would accept the score of students on their bar exams as evidence that they are ready to represent a defendant in a capital murder case. We would, as Wiggins and McTighe (2005) wisely suggest, require a broad range of evidence not only of their knowledge and professional competence but also of their empathy and understanding of others and themselves.

Second, we would provide feedback to professionals that not only assesses their present level of competence but also is designed to help them grow and learn. To what extent do contemporary teacher and leadership assessment systems meet this standard? In too many cases, assessments are absent, infrequent, ambiguous, and subjective (Reeves, 2009a). Any suggestion that the person being evaluated "needs improvement" is a dagger in the heart, an invitation to grievances and litigation, and a threat to faculty morale. It is therefore essential that school leaders distinguish evaluation—a process bounded by the constraints of legal precedent and collective bargaining—from assessment. The latter, as Stiggins suggests, need not be an adjudicatory process but should be focused on providing information designed to improve performance.

Third, schools can provide feedback to teachers and administrators in the form of a "preflight" checklist—that is, information and support before poor decisions adversely influence student achievement. Physicians, attorneys, and pilots, for example, routinely work with another professional close at hand before they wield the scalpel, conduct a cross-examination, or attempt a solo landing. Contrast that intense scrutiny to the typical experiences of student teachers and administrative interns. Indeed, the trend toward alternative certification programs seems destined to accentuate the "sink or swim" system, which would never be tolerated in the operating room, the courtroom, or the cockpit. But it is routinely tolerated and encouraged in the classroom and the principal's office, where the lives at stake are no less precious.

Fourth, we would provide low-risk, frequent, and constructive feedback that is designed to be formative. As Ainsworth and Viegut (2006) suggest in their description of common formative assessments for students, the feedback is consistent and purposeful, designed solely to improve performance.

Transforming Vision into Reality

A vision represents a compelling picture of the ideal state. In many educational systems, vision statements are thoughtful, if lofty, documents that represent the aspirations of the community. We envision a system in which all students will leave high school ready for additional education or the world of work. We foresee an educational environment in which every child learns every day. We can see, if only dimly, a future in which the inequities that afflict students outside of school are reduced to insignificance once they have crossed the threshold of the schoolhouse door. Based on the principles in this chapter, take a moment to consider how you can transform your vision into reality.

Initially, take a moment to think deeply about your present vision statement. If you do not have one, please do not wait for a committee meeting or the issuance of a board policy. Whatever your responsibilities are, describe in words your compelling picture of the ideal future state of your classroom, school, or system:

_____

_____

_____

Now apply each of the four elements of transforming vision into reality. First, describe the evidence that you would expect to see if the vision is fulfilled. Student test score results may be part of this body of evidence, but they are never the sole components of it. Consider evidence from each of the following areas:

Evidence of student results: _____

_____

Evidence of improved teacher practice: _____

_____

Evidence of improved leadership decisions: _____

_____

Evidence of system-level learning: _____

_____

Second, describe how you will provide assessment for learning for adults in the system. This is not a recapitulation of your formal evaluation system, but rather a mechanism that provides objective, fair, and safe feedback with the sole purpose of improving performance. Consider in particular each of the following groups:

Assessment for learning for teachers: _____

_____

Assessment for learning for building administrators: _____

_____

Assessment for learning for system administrators: _____

_____

Assessment for learning for policymakers: _____

_____

Assessment for learning for parents: _____

_____

Third, describe your preventive feedback—your preflight checklists—that you can use before decisions are made and before professional practices have had adverse influences on students:

Preflight checklist for teachers: _____

_____

Preflight checklist for building administrators: _____

_____

Preflight checklist for system administrators: _____

_____

Fourth, describe your formative feedback for a specific part of the vision. How will you provide information that is specific, constructive, and timely for teachers and administrators?

Timing of formative feedback: _____

_____

Content of formative feedback: _____

_____

Finally, return to the original vision statement—the compelling description of your ideal state. Now that you have considered the evidence and the context for this vision, can you provide greater clarity and specificity? The people reading your vision statement are earnest, hardworking, and sincerely engaged in the enterprise of teaching, leadership, and learning. But they simply don't know what you mean when you use vague expressions about educational excellence. Reconsider the vision and express it once again in the most clear and specific terms possible. Paint a picture with the words so that the newest staff members can grasp your hopes and dreams and can also understand their individual role in helping the system implement its vision.

Revised vision statement: _____

_____

In this chapter, we have proceeded from the general to the specific, transforming a lofty and worthy vision into evidence and actions for teachers, administrators, policymakers, and parents. In the next chapter, we continue to narrow the focus of high-impact learning through a concentration on the four areas that have the greatest effect on student achievement: teaching, curriculum, assessment, and leadership.

8

Focus: Teaching, Curriculum, Assessment, and Leadership

Goleman (2006) describes what for many of us is a normal day of intermittent interruptions, distractions, emergencies, and occasional attempts to engage in our intended work, conversations, and relationships. We are, he concludes,

> frazzled from the hassles of daily life. "Frazzle" is a neural state in which emotional upsurges hamper the workings of the executive center [of the brain]. While we are frazzled, we cannot concentrate or think clearly. That neural truth has direct implications for achieving the optimal emotional atmosphere both in the classroom and the office. From the vantage point of the brain, doing well in school and at work involves one and the same state, the brain's sweet spot for performance. The biology of anxiety casts us out of that zone for excellence. (p. 267)

Although some interruptions are beyond our control, Crenshaw (2008) argues that most of our attempts at multitasking are deliberate decisions that reduce our effectiveness. This chapter describes the powerful possibilities that open up to us when we reject the siren calls for personal and institutional fragmentation and instead focus on the essentials of teaching, curriculum, assessment, and leadership.

The Power of Focus

When we focus our attention in one area, we can reach a state of purposeful action that yields powerful emotional, physical, and professional results (Gallagher, 2009). On the other hand, multitasking behaviors resemble those of addicts who continue to feed their addiction long after their behavior provides pleasure or meets any physical or psychological need. Addicted multitaskers are physically uncomfortable and mentally distressed when removed from the multiple stimuli of electronic communications (usually many at the same time), simultaneous conversations, growing project and task lists, and frantic attempts to maintain personal relationships. Addicts ultimately face two choices: either they are liberated from the substance or behavior to which they are enslaved, or they succumb to their addiction, usually at great cost to themselves and those they profess to love. As anyone who has emerged on the other side of addiction can attest, the first alternative is far from easy but is certainly superior to the second.

Is it worth the effort? Do the benefits of focus outweigh the costs of enduring a painful separation from multitasking? First, we should acknowledge that multitasking does have benefits, though not the benefits that most people believe. The benefit is not efficiency, but the appearance of importance and the illusion of indispensability. These benefits are as real to the addicted multitasker as are the apparent glamour and sophistication of cigarette smoking to young nicotine addicts. We're not cancerous geezers with bad breath and nicotine-yellow fingertips, they think. We're Humphrey Bogart and Lauren Bacall.

Institutional multitasking also has its seductive appeal and short-term benefits. In his analysis of organizations that fell from spectacular success to disaster, Collins (2009) notes that one of the common characteristics of these failed organizations was that for many years they had been rewarded, financially and psychically, for their bad decisions. This led to "hubris born of success" (p. 27) followed by the "undisciplined pursuit of more" (p. 45). These behaviors are not unique to the corporate scene. In one school system I recently visited, the same document that claimed that the system possessed a laserlike focus on student achievement and that extolled the virtues of professional learning contained 117 separate professional learning initiatives in a single school year. Such fragmentation was deliberate; indeed, it was a source of pride in that particular system. The professional learning leaders left no doubt that they were very busy and important people with a thousand things to do. They thrive on fragmentation and will continue to do so until the costs of fragmentation exceed the benefits of focus.

If we expect individuals, schools, and systems to embrace focus, we must make a powerful case that the advantages are overwhelming. Loehr and Schwartz (2003) argue that the benefits of full engagement include exceptional levels of physical, emotional, mental, and spiritual energy for individuals. The pursuit of high-impact learning requires not only that we achieve individual and organizational focus, but also that we focus on the right things: teaching, curriculum, assessment, and leadership.

Focus on Teaching

The impact of effective teaching on student achievement is well documented (Hattie, 2009; Marzano, 2007). Unfortunately, the pursuit of effective teaching strategies in an unfocused way has the opposite effect of what is intended. Some states have established official observation protocols that require administrators to check off each effective strategy that they observe, implying that an effective classroom teacher would bounce like the silver ball in a pinball machine, from hypothesis testing to comparisons to nonlinguistic representations. Teachers respond to an increasing list of diverse demands not with greater effectiveness but with weariness, mistrust, and disengagement (Hargreaves, 2007). The only comic relief for them might be when they notice that the district staff development catalog has added a 118th seminar, the one about the importance of focus for teachers and principals.

A focus on effective teaching, therefore, is not about workshops or checklists, but about deliberate practice. Willingham (2009) notes that "teaching, like any complex cognitive skill, must be practiced to be improved" (p. 147). As we noted in Chapter 6, a consensus of scientific evidence in a variety of domains, including athletics, music, decision making, and chess, to name a few, concludes that deliberate practice is the key to improved performance (Ericsson et al., 2006). The components of deliberate practice include performance that is focused on a particular element of the task, expert coaching, feedback, careful and accurate self-assessment, and—this is the key—the opportunity to apply feedback immediately for improved performance.

But deliberate practice is far from the professional learning model provided to teachers. Often professional learning activities are characterized by a series of one-way transmissions. If there is any pretense toward interaction, it is limited to the suggestion that participants discuss what they have learned from the past 20 minutes of uninterrupted transmission of information.

High-impact learning requires a radical transformation from transmission to focus and deliberate practice. For example, Willingham (2009) suggests that teachers videotape their lessons and then watch the tapes alone and with a colleague, and after careful review, identify specific opportunities for improvement in professional practice. He cautions:

> It's not productive just to sit down and watch them like a movie, waiting to see what will happen. You should have a concrete goal, such as observing classroom management or observing the emotional atmosphere of the classroom.... *The point of this exercise is not to "spot the flaw."* [Comments] should be concrete and about the behaviors you observe, not about the qualities you infer.... The purpose of watching your partner teach is to help her reflect on her practice, to think about her teaching. You do that by describing what you see. (pp. 155–156, emphasis in original)

Contrast the intensity of this experience to the passive scenario of most meetings, conferences, and workshops. Deliberate practice is potentially stressful and draining, but it is far more productive than the practice-free environment of typical seminars.

The time required for focused professional learning is extraordinary, at least in the context of most current schedules. Darling-Hammond and Richardson (2009) synthesized professional learning research and noted:

> Teachers who had 80 or more hours of professional development in inquiry-based science during the previous year were significantly more likely to use this type of science instruction than teachers who had experienced fewer hours.... Studies of professional development lasting 14 or fewer hours showed no effects on student learning.... The largest effects were found for programs offering between 30 and 100 hours spread out over 6–12 months. (p. 49)

Although this sort of commitment may sound overwhelming in a time of tight budgets and crammed schedules, trade-offs are possible. What would be the effect on professional learning if you combined the traditional opening-of-school inspirational speech, four district-level staff development days, and 18 biweekly staff meetings—perhaps 48 hours of professional learning—and focused all of them on improved literacy instruction? While your immediate thoughts might migrate to all of the content that teachers would miss by forgoing those workshops and meetings, weigh that loss against the power of focus on a single area of improved teaching. To make the comparison more dramatic, stop for a moment and evaluate the effect on learning of the school opening, the one-day workshops, and the staff meetings of last year. What aspects of that content are you applying? What would you have missed by being absent those days? If you were to decide in the months ahead to substitute high-impact learning for meetings, assemblies, and workshops, you may decide that you are not giving up very much after all.

Focus on Curriculum and Assessment

Although a focus on teaching strategies is important, a commitment to high-impact learning also requires that we consider the content of what is taught. In fewer than 15 years, the number of states with academic content standards expanded from 12 to 50. In many schools around the globe, curriculum has grown in scope and complexity. In mathematics and science in particular, the curriculum that was previously addressed in the middle grades has migrated to upper-elementary years. Thus elementary school educators with little or no formal mathematics background have been required to understand algebra with the depth required to teach pre-algebra skills in grades 4 and 5, often with little more support than a new set of textbooks.

A focus on curriculum alone, however, is insufficient. Rather, high-impact learning must include an explicit integration of what is to be taught and how essential learning will be assessed. One of the most powerful ways to deepen teacher understanding of standards and curriculum is the following five-step process that helps teachers focus on the most important part of each curriculum area and then gain a deep understanding through a comprehensive assessment development process.

First, teachers identify the most important elements of the curriculum by applying the criteria of leverage, endurance, and importance for the next level of instruction. By leverage, we mean the applicability of the knowledge and skills required of students to other disciplines. By endurance, we mean the extent to which student knowledge is sustained over time. The importance for the next level of instruction can be evaluated best through a dialog with colleagues who are teaching higher grade levels. When confronted with dozens of curriculum elements, it is difficult to know where to start, but by applying these three criteria, teachers can focus on what is most important as they continue the rest of this powerful process.

Second, teachers collaborate to create new performance assessments, including specific scoring guides that evaluate each level of student performance. This requirement is substantially different than writing test items or creating brief problems. A performance assessment is a multistep set of engaging tasks that builds knowledge and provides incremental feedback for students. Students do not proceed to the third step until they have achieved proficiency in the first two steps. This is the same "deliberate practice" for students that the research supports for adult learning. This process is described more fully in *Making Standards Work* (Reeves, 2002c).

Third, teachers work alone to provide what they believe are exemplary responses for each task in the performance assessment. This step is sometimes met with resistance. Why would we ask a college-educated adult to complete a performance task designed for students who haven't finished high school? What can possibly be gained by completing a 3rd grade assignment? If you will suspend disbelief and engage in the experiment, however, it will soon become apparent that a dozen well-educated and thoroughly professional teachers can develop at least a dozen different responses to the same directions on an assessment.

Fourth, exchange papers and apply the scoring rubrics created in the second step to the work of a colleague. This is ideally done with several teams working in parallel, so that the papers can be exchanged anonymously. All you have in this step is a scoring rubric and several pieces of "student" work that were created with the intent of achieving the highest possible score. The point of this step, however, is really not the evaluation of the work of a colleague. The real object of evaluation is the scoring rubric. Inevitably there are areas of ambiguity that lead to the uncomfortable experience of professionals with graduate degrees failing to understand a teacher's intent on the assessment.

Fifth, return to the assessment instructions and scoring rubrics and revise them to remove ambiguities and create the maximum opportunity for student success. We create these opportunities not through easy requirements or a reduction of rigor, but rather through explicit instructions and clear standards of success.

This process seems exhaustive, and it could require years to apply it to every element of the curriculum. Stigler and Hiebert (1999) acknowledge similar challenges to the development of effective lesson plans. Five years might elapse, challengers contended, before such a detailed process could be applied to every subject. But five years will come and go whether or not we have an improved understanding of curriculum and assessments. Therefore, it is all the more important that teachers focus precious professional learning time on the elements of the curriculum that are most important, that they develop deep understanding of the curriculum by creating and performing assessment tasks, and that they engage in a process of continued refinement and improvement of their professional practices and the assessments that they use in the classroom.

Focus on Leadership

Although teachers have an undeniably large influence on student results, they are able to maximize that influence only when they are supported by school and system leaders who give them the time, the professional learning opportunities, and the respect that are essential for effective teaching. This begins with processes for effective feedback to support instruction. Note well that feedback is not the same as evaluation, a process that seems dedicated to the proposition that professional practices cannot be improved. As DuFour and Marzano (2009) note, "The odds are far greater that a tenured teacher would be struck by lightning during his or her lifetime than found to be an ineffective teacher" (p. 64). Moreover, they observe that secondary school administrators cannot possibly have the content area expertise to evaluate the curriculum and assessment knowledge of every teacher in a school. Therefore, the systemic focus on effective leadership that is designed to maximize the impact of teaching on student learning must emphasize neither evaluation nor a fire hose of content. Rather, leaders must be the architects of systems and schedules that lead to professional learning.

Leadership focus includes three essential elements. First, leaders remain fixated on the fact that student achievement is the criterion for evaluating teaching, the curriculum, and assessment strategies. This is the opposite of consumer-driven professional learning, in which teaching professionals select courses and conferences from catalogs. With relentless regularity, focused leaders ask the question "Is it working to improve student learning?" Every other leadership decision that they make must be seen through the lens of the effect on student learning. This focus includes seemingly mundane decisions about student assemblies, faculty meetings, and extracurricular activities; all can have a positive, neutral, or negative effect on student achievement, and every leadership decision requires careful evaluation from that perspective.

Second, leaders focus on equity of educational opportunity through common curriculum and assessments. Distributing standards and inspecting curriculum and lesson planning notebooks are not enough. Until a school has common formative assessments that provide evidence of common expectations for every student in the same class in the same grade, learning opportunities and expectations will remain wildly varied from one classroom to the next. It is not enough to create opportunities for workshops or to label staff meetings as "professional learning communities." Leaders must establish clear targets for the content, frequency, and review of formative assessments.

Third, leaders focus on developing other leaders. This aspect of focused leadership does not imply only the identification and promotion of administrators, though that is surely an important responsibility of system-level leaders. Sustained capacity building for high-impact learning depends upon the development of teacher leadership. Successful teaching focus, including deliberate practice, videotaping, and incremental improvement in the art and science of teaching, depends upon teacher leaders who provide feedback to help their colleagues and who receive feedback on the impact of their coaching.

I am not unaware that school and system-level leaders are preoccupied with many other demands. Buses, buildings, and school boards are among those responsibilities that can drain time and energy from leaders who would prefer to support teachers but have to deal with a discipline hearing, a grievance, and a parent complaint in the next 30 minutes. These exigencies cannot be ignored, but they render all the more important the choices in how leaders invest their time. Moreover, the multiple demands on leaders make clear that they must keep the focus on teaching and learning. Because administrators cannot do this alone, they must make maximum use of teacher leaders. One of the most powerful ways that teachers influence their peers is the application of action research, the subject we consider in the next chapter.

9

Making Action Research Work

Too often there is a false dichotomy in the research literature between "real" research (that is, double-blind experimental studies with random assignment of students to control and treatment groups) and the rest of the field—case studies, qualitative descriptions, and action research. The first is rigorous; the others are casual. The first is objective; the others suffer from the subjective biases of the researchers. The first is independent; the others are subject to the influences of bonds that grow between the researcher and the students and teachers who are being studied. In this chapter we explore the reasons that these comparisons are somewhat beside the point. Of course we need rigorous quantitative research in order to draw inferences that can be generalized to large populations. We also need the stories behind the numbers, the qualitative lens through which we can better understand quantitative information. And educators in particular need to see a demonstration of practical application in a local environment, because they have seen too many programs that claimed to be "research-based" and that were colossal wastes of money and time. In sum, we must use the combination of different research methods to influence teachers and educational leaders to improve their practices.

Influencing Professional Practices

Gabriel (2005, p. x) suggests that teacher leaders have four responsibilities: "influencing school culture, building and maintaining a successful team, equipping other potential teacher leaders, and enhancing or improving student achievement." My previous research on the subject (Reeves, 2008) concluded that "teachers not only exert significant influence on the performance of students, but they also influence the performance of other teachers and school leaders" (p. 2). The source of influence is not a position, such as department head, or a designation, such as instructional coach. The source of influence is rather the systematic observation of the impact of specific teaching practices on student achievement and the continuous sharing of those observations with colleagues.

Goldsmith, Morgan, and Ogg (2004) make the compelling point that business and nonprofit organizations are, like schools, drowning in data but continue to make poor decisions for want of practical information that is readily usable by organizational leaders. They make a compelling argument for complementary research methods, including experiential and experimental research, in some surprising contexts. When decisions are judgment calls without a clear cause and effect, it is easy to prefer gut feelings over hard data. But when decisions involve life and death, as they do in pharmaceutical and medical research, there might seem to be little opportunity for judgment. Nevertheless, the authors demonstrate that some of the best new ideas are emerging from collaborative and alternative approaches to research.

Consider the case of nonfiction writing, a powerful cross-disciplinary strategy that has consistently been linked to improved student achievement in reading comprehension, mathematics, science, and social studies (Bangert-Drowns, Hurley, & Wilkinson, 2004; Reeves, 2002a). It is an established fact that a majority of students in the United States need improved writing skills and that our failure to respond to this evidence causes employers and colleges to spend billions of dollars to address writing deficiencies. Where has that overwhelming quantitative case led? Kiuhara, Graham, and Hawken (2009) conducted a national study on the teaching of writing to high school students and found that evidence-based teaching practices to support writing were insufficiently used with any degree of frequency and depth. The teachers in the study claimed that they had not been sufficiently trained to teach writing, with the percentage of teachers believing that they were ill prepared in this subject directly related to their failure to apply writing strategies in the classroom. In other words, teachers do not do what they do not know.

The immediate rejoinder might be that teachers *do* know what they should do—the research has been around for a long time, and it would require deliberate indifference to avoid it. Such frustration often leads to administrative imperatives that only compound the problem. A better approach, one that resulted in both measurable increases in the teaching of writing and improved student results, occurred when teachers in Clark County, Nevada, combined the available quantitative studies on the impact of writing with their own action research projects. Teachers and principals who had been aware of the power of writing on improved student achievement for several years were impelled to action not by virtue of another study establishing the same conclusions, but rather because of action research in which their teaching colleagues demonstrated that the research was relevant and effective in the local context.

Strengths and Weaknesses of Action Research

Enthusiasm for action research, particularly when conducted by teachers, must be tempered with an acknowledgment of its limitations. The most obvious limitation is that the researcher is clearly biased. No professional educators would engage deliberately in instructional practices that they expected to fail. Indeed, part of their professional responsibility is to make midcourse corrections, to provide differentiated instructional strategies and deliberately unequal time in order to meet student needs. These are hardly standard experimental conditions from which scientific inferences can be made. Moreover, the actual practice of action research includes a good deal of opinion and rhetoric that may not directly stem from the observations. Some of the published action research is overtly political and burdened with extended comments from the research subjects, who are presumed to be authorities by virtue of the coincidence that they were participants in the study at hand.

In a nuanced editorial in the *Journal of Educational Psychology*, Graesser (2009) noted, "It is important for the field of educational psychology to maintain its scientific integrity" but added that "educational settings are inherently complex, so there is a delicate balance between preserving the methodological rigor of our research designs and testing the students in ecologically valid learning environments" (p. 259). There are also ethical issues in our search for methodological rigor, particularly in the use of random assignments to control groups and to experimental groups, precisely the opposite of evidence of concern for individual student needs (Reeves, 2002b).

Moreover, even the most meticulous quantitative measurement does not necessarily support an inference of causality. Correlations, even when carried out to three decimal points and explained in the Greek argot of statistical analyses, are still correlations. As Kachigan (1986) notes:

> While in most analyses the implications are quite clear, there are instances in which the interpretation may vary from individual to individual. At this point, the analysis becomes an art as well as a science. So it is best to think of the interpretation issue as belonging on a continuum, with statistical analysis on one end and art, tea leaf reading, astrology, and crystal ball gazing at the other extreme. (p. 11)

Action research, therefore, is not a substitute for quantitative research, but a contextual lens for other research. Graesser issues the profound challenge to researchers of every orientation that they "quantify the qualitative data. Researchers also qualify the quantitative data by collecting verbal protocols in tandem with quantitative measures to assess the validity of the measures or to perform manipulation checks on the interventions. These are established scientific methods of integrating qualitative and quantitative analyses" (p. 261). He cautions, however, that we should be skeptical of studies that reflect selective cases that serve only to illustrate the writer's bias.

This is the central dilemma of action research. We all do have biases, so the choice is not the presence or absence of biases but rather the extent to which we admit them forthrightly and admit when the evidence fails to confirm our biases. I have had to publicly eat crow when I submitted titles of presentations before my research was complete, only to find that the evidence undermined my title (Reeves, 2006b). The title, published in a conference manual, was "The Multiple Intelligences of Leadership." What could possibly go wrong? Howard Gardner is a rock star, multiple intelligences is a framework that is widely acknowledged, and I was going to take it a step further in my application to educational leadership. There were only two problems: I was wrong about the theory and wrong about the evidence. I then had the pleasure of telling about a thousand people who came to hear about the multiple intelligences of leadership that I was sorry to disappoint them, but I was wrong, and that I had some other research that I hoped they would find useful. Professional learning does not advance, however, through the inexorable confirmation of previous certainties, but through a systematic challenge to our present conceptions. As Will Rogers reminded us, "It's not what a fellow don't know that bothers me. It's what he knows for sure that just ain't so."

School leaders have a particular responsibility to recognize and respect research integrity, particularly when a teacher-researcher expresses disappointment that a planned intervention was ineffective. Rather than a disappointment, such a finding is useful to help all of us reconsider our previous attitudes and beliefs. Our search must be not only for "what works" and celebrations of success but also for professional learning, and that occurs when we fail as well as when we succeed. Indeed, the evidence discussed earlier on deliberate practice suggests that the optimal zone of performance improvement occurs when we are not succeeding, but failing.

The pianist who knows a Chopin prelude by memory and plays it daily may enjoy the experience but will never advance to an etude by the same composer. Teachers who are similarly confident and comfortable with a particular lesson plan and teaching style will not improve engagement or student learning unless they try, and fail, in pursuit of better strategies.

In sum, educators and school leaders must encourage colleagues to conduct research and to accept discomfiting information. For example, people who loathe testing have a great deal of difficulty with evidence that frequent assessment improves learning, just as people like me who avoid most cardiovascular exercises and who enjoy the taste of deep-fried anything in barbeque sauce do not appreciate the research evidence that suggests that these choices may not be associated with optimal health. Our discussions of research would, however, be more productive if every professional were willing to reconsider previous preferences and tastes and engage in experiments of alternative practices based on new data. This will not necessarily be comfortable—I will still prefer onion rings to celery sticks—but it will be necessary if we wish to use research to make improvements.

Removing Obstacles to Teacher Leadership

There are four common barriers to teacher leadership. The first is toxic hierarchy. Schools are hierarchical systems, as are most organizations. Even those enterprises that pride themselves on the absence of titles and bosses and the presence of pervasive egalitarianism still have accountability relationships, or they do not remain viable. The challenge, therefore, is not the removal of hierarchy but rather the supplementation of hierarchy with effective networks (Fink & Hargreaves, 2006; Reeves, 2009c). In his quest to identify the "moon shots" of leadership for the 21st century, Hamel (2009) noted that one of the five central challenges of the coming decades will be the displacement of the toxic elements of hierarchy, including wildly disproportionate rewards, distorted senses of entitlement, and immunization from criticism.

The second barrier to teacher leadership is the compliance orientation that pervades many school systems. Much of this is a reaction to the
anarchy that ensued when school systems embraced site-based management beyond any threshold of logic and reason. Marzano and Waters (2009)
concluded that our reaction to chaos should not be a return to Stalinist centralization but rather what they call "defined autonomy." They explained
the paradox in this way:

> On one hand, we found evidence that school autonomy has a positive rela-
> tionship with student achievement. On the other hand, we found little or
> no relationship between site-based management and student achievement.
> This seeming paradox is rendered less mysterious through the construct of
> defined autonomy. While it is true that schools are unique and must oper-
> ate in such a way as to address their unique needs, it is also true that each
> school must operate as a functional component of a larger system. It is the
> larger system—the district—that establishes the common work of schools
> within the district, and it is that common work that becomes the "glue"
> holding the district together. (pp. 89–90)

We might put this balance into operation within the framework of a balanced accountability system that includes system-level requirements in
one tier of indicators, and school-based indicators—chosen by school
administrators and teachers based on the particular needs of that school—
in the second tier of accountability indicators (Reeves, 2004a). Compliance is not without its merits—school safety depends on compliance with
standards for lead paint, playground equipment, and crosswalk guards.
Similarly, there should be essential systemwide standards for instruction,
covering everything ranging from the avoidance of corporal punishment to
the embrace of formative assessment. But the ultimate test of effectiveness
is not mere compliance, best illustrated by the "I taught it; they just didn't
learn it" syndrome. The test of effectiveness is a balanced combination of
documented improvements in student learning and professional practices.

The third barrier to teacher leadership is the common practice of
shooting the messenger. Classroom teachers who point out that some educational reforms embraced by school leaders lack evidentiary support are

targeted as change resisters who just don't get it. Change is difficult and opposition is inevitable. But not all opposition to change is based on an irrational and perverse commitment to poor results. Indeed, an educational system committed to continuous improvement should welcome a particular sort of resistance—based not on personal attacks on the advocates of change but on an ethic of hypothesis testing. "You believe that children will learn to read naturally without wasting time on letter sounds? That's an interesting hypothesis; let's test it." "You believe that teaching students to learn math facts is a notion rendered meaningless by the availability of calculators? No problem, let's compare the performance of two groups of students and examine which one is better prepared for advanced concepts in mathematics and science." I cannot recall hearing such a rational discourse in the reading and math wars of the past three decades, as hypothesis testing was often displaced by bitter recriminations by the true believers on all sides. In the future, some instructional, technological, and leadership innovations will work and some will fail. We will make more progress, at a greatly accelerated rate, when change advocates and resisters commit themselves to a discipline of exchanging alternative hypotheses rather than hand grenades.

This issue is closely related to the fourth barrier to teacher leadership, and that is disrespect. Jonathan Jansen (2009) was the first black dean of education at the formerly all-white University of Pretoria in South Africa. Though the change from apartheid-based minority rule to democracy may strike some readers as an extreme example, Jansen's perceptions about the highly charged interrelationships between emotions, politics, and behaviors offer important insights for leaders at every level. He notes that "educational change is combustible at the point where politics and emotions meet" (p. 198), and it certainly does not require a change as dramatic as South Africa's to recognize the barrier that fundamental disrespect creates for teacher leadership.

In the context of professional learning, respect is conveyed when teachers are participants in, not merely consumers of, research and the professional learning that accompanies it. Respect is also demonstrated when teachers are challenged rather than coddled. The prevailing hypothesis among some leaders is that they should not ask teachers to engage in more effective practices because they are already so overwhelmed that it will push them over the edge. Carbonneau, Vallerand, Fernet, and Guay (2008) demonstrate that what teachers most need is not the absence of professional demands but passionate engagement in which they find meaning and purpose. Just as high expectations of students are consistently linked to improved performance, teachers also benefit from the expectation that they can and will have a profound effect on the lives of students and colleagues.

A Model for Action Research

Although action research protocols can be very formal, the following model was tested with 81 teams of teachers and administrators (Reeves, 2008), and the results suggested that it not only was widely applied and replicated by teachers but also had a positive effect on student achievement in more than two-thirds of the action research projects in which it was used. The model includes the following elements:

• **Research question**—This is an inquiry about a particular link between professional practices and student results. For example, how will interactive journals influence the writing performance of second-language students in a 7th grade math class?

• **Student population**—This is a description of the grade levels and special characteristics of the students participating in the project. Although action research makes no pretense of randomly selected subjects, it is nevertheless important for reviewers of research to understand the demographic and educational factors that might influence the research findings.

• **Student achievement data**—This includes data not only from year-end tests but also from formative assessments, classroom observations, and other instruments that allow for a systematic observation of changes in student achievement. It is most effective if there are several measurements throughout an action research project so that student absences on a single test day do not have a distorting effect on the results.

• **Professional practices to be observed**—This is the missing link in most action research projects and offers the greatest opportunities for teachers to bring more descriptive rigor to their reflections on professional practices. Terms such as "collaborative learning" or "differentiated instruction" have little meaning without clear specifications. Ideally, the action researchers will create a scoring rubric with a range of performance over three or four different levels so that an objective observation can be made about the extent to which a particular practice was applied in the classroom. The claim that "we used high-yield instructional strategies" is far less helpful than "we changed the interval of feedback from four times on 30-item tests to twelve times on 10-item tests and shortened the feedback loop from three days to the same day."

We now turn our attention to sustaining high-impact learning. What have we learned about the impact on student achievement of effective professional learning over time? Part 3 moves the discussion beyond the traditional "train the trainer" model that sustains poor practice more than organizational learning. Instead, we consider a combination of strategies that encompass assessment, ownership, and coaching.

PART 3:

How to Sustain
High-Impact
Professional Learning

10

Beyond "Train the Trainer"

The term *train* disturbs educators for a variety of reasons. "Monkeys are trained," they complain, "and professionals are developed." Nevertheless, the term remains in active use in many school systems to refer to methods used to change the behavior of children and teachers. We train teachers to stand in line and be well behaved, and we train children to use a new curriculum—or is it the other way around?

An excursion into the *Shorter Oxford English Dictionary* explains why our visceral distaste for training is well founded. The noun *train* comes from the Old French *traine*, connoting "guile, deceit, ruse" and is defined as "an act or scheme designed to deceive or entrap someone; a trick, a stratagem." Wait—it gets better. As a verb, the first definition of *train* is "draw or pull along; drag, haul." As a transitive verb it means "drag out, protract, spin out; spend or pass time slowly or tediously." Were the Oxford etymologists recent participants in staff development seminars? We must slog through to the sixth definition to get anywhere close to the definition that most educational leaders intend when they ask someone to "train our teachers." The sixth definition starts well enough: "Provide (especially a young person) with a moral and disciplined upbringing; educate, rear." But our original fears are soon validated as we wade deeper into the Oxford pool. The definition continues: "Discipline and teach (an animal) to obey orders or perform tricks; school and prepare (a horse, especially a racehorse) for competition."

Oxford is no more encouraging in its definition of *trainer*: "A person who trains or instructs a person or animal; an instructor; a person who trains athletes, footballers, racehorses, etc., as a profession. Also, a piece of equipment used for training; an exercise machine" (pp. 3,320–3,321). Suddenly the phrase "train the trainer" is a compound expression for the very worst in professional learning. In this chapter we explore how schools and educational systems can break free of this counterproductive notion and create a new vision for building capacity for high-impact learning.

Essentials for Sustainable Improvement

Fullan (2005, p. 14) suggests that sustainability has eight elements:

1. Public service with a moral purpose
2. Commitment to changing context at all levels
3. Lateral capacity building through networks
4. Intelligent accountability and vertical relationships (encompassing both capacity building and accountability)
5. Deep learning
6. Dual commitment to short-term and long-term results
7. Cyclical energizing
8. The long lever of leadership

Fullan adds that "systems thinking in practice ... is the key to sustainability" (p. 43) and argues that leaders must amplify their learning with experience. As a general leadership principle, however, the longer the list of things to be done and criteria to be met, the lower the probability that the list will be accomplished. That's why at least a few people still read Immanuel Kant (1785); the Categorical Imperative is a very short list indeed, with a single nonnegotiable moral mandate. But outside of the philosopher's world, being right is not sufficient. We must be both right and effective, a quality that Fullan finds to be inconsistent with moral superiority and judgmentalism. He therefore suggests three criteria for building capacity for change: competencies, resources, and motivation; and he notes that

> individuals and groups are high in capacity if they possess and continue to develop knowledge and skills, if they attract and use resources (time, ideas, expertise, money) wisely, and if they are committed to putting in the energy to get important things done *collectively* and *continuously* (ever learning). This is a tall order in complex systems, but it is exactly the order required. (2008, p. 57, emphasis in original)

How can we reconcile Kantian imperatives with Fullan's practicality? The answer lies in a careful distinction between imperatives and influence. Although imperatives appear to have the rhetorical and moral high ground, influence is what changes personal behavior and organizational performance. Patterson and colleagues (2008) identified six sources of influence on changing behavior in highly technical professionals, such as surgeons, as well as drug addicts, convicts, and matriarchs in a remote African village who carried tainted water to their villages. It is noteworthy that neither policy memoranda nor inspirational seminars were the solution for any of these groups, any more than they are for educational systems. Influence is the result of a combination of personal motivation and ability, social motivation and ability, and structural motivation and ability.

Organizations seeking influence—that is, sustainable improvements in individual and organizational effectiveness—must not only harness the power of the individual, social, and structural elements of influence; they must also take care to avoid or eliminate counterproductive influences. For example, school systems might do a fine job of creating individual and social motivation and ability to promote improved teaching but undermine those efforts with structural deficits in motivation and ability. The seminars, speeches, and informal conversations may all support formative assessment, while the structural evaluation processes consider only summative evaluation. Individual and social motivation may seek to promote effective teaching and leadership, while the structural elements of the environment consider only test scores of students and dismiss the data concerning the actions of teachers and leaders that were the antecedents to student results.

Influence is, in sum, much like teaching. It does not stem from a single person, whether the classroom teacher or the organizational leader. It requires the development of individual and social abilities, something that comes with deliberate practice and feedback. Influence and teaching also occur within an environment that may either promote or denigrate these efforts.

Sustaining People and Practices

Sustainability is more than a victory in an endurance contest. Even an ill-trained fried-food addict can finish a marathon or climb the Grand Teton, but in my case these accomplishments are greater testimony to my irra-tional persistence than to the sustainability of these efforts. True sustain-ability requires a double-edged focus on people and practices. People need to be respected more than they need to win the favor of their supervisors or secure a victory in organizational politics. Kim and Mauborgne (2003) found that employees were far more satisfied in situations in which they initially disagreed with a leadership decision but were then persuaded that the process used in reaching the decision was fair, than if the decision itself was acceptable but the process was unfair. Casciaro and Lobo (2005) concluded that no matter how competent people are, if they behave in an inappropriate and offensive manner that undermines their colleagues, their influence will be minimal as the effect of their behavior undermines the value of their knowledge. Sutton (2007) bolsters the argument in a more scatological but equally effective manner.

Maslow's hierarchy may have served our primitive ancestors—or at least those occupying leadership positions in the 20th century—well. But today, respect and human decency are the currency of the realm. While we take food, shelter, and safety for granted in most cases, the new basic need is for meaning, worth, and respect. Leaders should end every day by asking themselves, if they have sufficient time for only a letter of reprimand or a letter of commendation, which alternative will yield the greatest influence? It's not a close call.

In the next chapter we consider how to translate leadership influence into assessments for teachers and administrators. We already know what ineffective assessment looks like, and most readers need only consider their most recent performance review for evidence on this point. Fortunately, there are constructive alternatives that we will now explore.

11

Performance Assessment for Teachers and Administrators

James Popham, one of the leading assessment experts of the last four decades, is more than casually upset with the routine abuse of the term *formative assessment* in schools. It is not a test or an event, he argues, but a process designed to improve learning. He offers the following specific definition:

> Formative assessment is a planned process in which assessment-elicited evidence of students' status is used by teachers to adjust their ongoing instructional procedures or by students to adjust their current learning tactics. (2008, p. 6)

In this chapter we explore the application of these principles to the assessment of learning for teachers, school leaders, and instructional teams. As Popham suggests, effective formative assessment is designed to promote learning, not merely to render an evaluation. It is a reciprocal process, influencing both the teacher and the learner.

This chapter refers to three sources of performance assessment systems. A new alternative for teacher assessment is provided by Marshall (2010); it has a history of direct application for both formative and summative feedback to teachers in a highly unionized environment. The Leadership Performance Matrix (Reeves, 2009a) suggests a comprehensive framework for providing formative feedback to administrators. Finally, Appendix B of this book contains a system that can be used for formative and summative evaluation for school teams engaged in planning, implementation, and monitoring processes. The particular advantage of the last assessment is that it has been independently linked (Fernandez, 2006) to gains in student achievement.

New Directions in Teacher Assessment

One of the most vexing challenges for teachers and school administrators is the teacher evaluation process. Too often the formal observation is distorted by the observers themselves, who announce their visit in advance in an atmosphere of extraordinary stress and anxiety for nontenured teachers. At the other extreme is the present vogue of "walk-throughs," which can seem casual and superficial, particularly when the observer is unclear about the expectations of the process. Walk-throughs can be effective, but they represent another case of the label being an insufficient guarantee of success. Marshall's new teacher evaluation rubrics seek to remedy this dilemma. Although the stakes can be high—he has used an earlier version of these evaluation forms, with the approval of the Boston Teachers Union, for formal teacher evaluation—the rubrics can also serve as an effective learning tool and formative assessment for teachers and administrators. The key to their utility is their exceptional specificity and consistency.

The new rubrics are organized around six domains: planning and preparation for learning; classroom management; delivery of instruction; monitoring, assessment, and follow-up; family and community outreach; and professional responsibilities. For each domain, a detailed rubric describes performance at four levels: "expert," "proficient," "needs improvement," and "does not meet standards." For example, the domain of planning and preparation for learning covers 10 specific areas, including knowledge, strategy, alignment, assessments, anticipation, lessons, engagement, materials, differentiation, and environment. Here is the range of performance for "differentiation":

- **Expert**—Designs lessons that break down complex tasks and addresses all learning needs, styles, and interests.
- **Proficient**—Designs lessons that target diverse learning needs, styles, and interests.
- **Needs improvement**—Plans lessons with some thought as to how to accommodate special needs students.
- **Does not meet standards**—Plans lessons aimed at the "middle" of the class.

The domain of classroom management includes 10 specific areas of focus, one of which is "expectations." The range of performance includes the following descriptions:

- **Expert**—Is direct, specific, consistent, and tenacious in communicating and enforcing very high expectations.
- **Proficient**—Clearly communicates and consistently enforces high standards for student behavior.
- **Needs improvement**—Announces and posts classroom rules and punishments.
- **Does not meet standards**—Comes up with ad hoc rules and punishments as events unfold during the year.

One final example completes the illustration of the value of specificity in the use of rubrics as formative feedback for improving teaching quality. For "incentives," within the domain of classroom management, the range of performance includes the following:

- **Expert**—Gets students to buy into a highly effective system of incentives linked to intrinsic rewards.
- **Proficient**—Uses incentives wisely to encourage and reinforce student cooperation.

- **Needs improvement**—Uses extrinsic rewards in an attempt to get students to cooperate and comply.
- **Does not meet standards**—Gives away "goodies" (e.g., free time) without using it as a lever to improve behavior.

In each of these examples, the teachers receiving feedback have a clear road map for improvement. They know in precise detail not only where they stand but also what specific professional practices they must pursue in order to improve. All of the observations are based on specific behavior, not a subjective opinion that includes words such as *excellent* and *above average*, which are typically part of a nearly meaningless range of descriptions in many teacher observation forms.

The rubrics cover a range of performance, providing a more nuanced and accurate reflection of reality than the binary (*yes* or *no, present* or *absent*) checklists that are sometimes used in the classroom walk-through process. Most important, this instrument is designed to improve performance. Indeed, within the domain of monitoring, assessment, and follow-up, there are clear expectations for reflection, with expert performance described as follows: "Works with colleagues to reflect on what worked and what didn't and continuously improves instruction." This is in contrast to "When a teaching unit or lesson doesn't go well, chalks it up to experience."

The complete rubrics are available as an open-source document. Although instructional teams may wish to modify the wording of these rubrics to better meet their needs, the structure, clarity, specificity, and learning orientation of this work provide an excellent model, particularly when compared to prevailing methods of teaching evaluation and formative assessment.

Alternatives for Leadership Assessment

The Leadership Performance Matrix (Reeves, 2009a) considers 10 domains of educational leadership: resilience, personal behavior, student achievement,

decision making, communication, faculty development, leadership development, time/task/project management, technology, and learning. The matrix
is based on a national study of leadership evaluations. As with the teaching
rubric, the Leadership Performance Matrix can be used to provide explicit
formative feedback to school leaders at the school and system levels and
also to create a roadmap for improvement. Of particular relevance to the
quest for high-impact learning is Dimension 10.3, professional development
focus. Here are the descriptions of the levels for this dimension:

• **Exemplary (systemwide impact)**—Can identify specific professional
development offerings of past years that have been systematically reviewed
and terminated because they failed to support organizational goals. Has
a process for prior review of new professional development programs
and rigorously applies its applications for time and funding. Can provide
examples of having disapproved applications for professional development that failed to meet these criteria. Chooses one or two focus areas for
professional development, with extensive time in faculty meetings, grade-
level meetings, department meetings, and staff development meetings all
focused on intensive implementation of a few areas of learning.

• **Proficient (local impact)**—Professional plan has no more than six
areas of emphasis and each of those areas is linked to the organization's
strategic objective.

• **Progressing (leadership potential)**—Professional development
opportunities are somewhat related to the organizational objective, but
there is no way of systematically assessing their impact. Participant evaluations are the primary criteria for selection, so programs that are popular
but ineffective tend to be the norm.

• **Not meeting standards**—By personal example, this leader endorses
the butterfly approach to professional development. Once a subject has
been superficially addressed, then a new fad is chased. Faculty requests
are routinely approved whether or not they are related to student achievement. Similarly, the leader's personal professional development agenda is
based on whim and preference, not organizational needs.

Within the domain of faculty development, the following range of performance is specified for "personal participation in leading professional development":

- **Exemplary (systemwide impact)**—In addition to meeting the criteria for "Proficient," the leader is also an active participant in teacher-led professional development, demonstrating with a commitment of time and intellect that the leader is a learner and is willing to learn from colleagues on a regular basis. The leader routinely shares learning experiences with other leaders and colleagues throughout the system.
- **Proficient (local impact)**—The leader devotes faculty meetings to professional development, not announcements. The leader personally leads professional development several times a year.
- **Progressing (leadership potential)**—The leader sometimes devotes faculty meetings to professional development and occasionally shares personal learning experiences with colleagues.
- **Not meeting standards**—The leader generally stopped acquiring new information after completing graduate school and displays little or no evidence of new learning or sharing that learning with colleagues.

In actual applications in school systems, the Leadership Performance Matrix has added elements of clarity, specificity, and fairness that are rare in administrator assessment. The study from which the matrix was developed revealed that 18 percent of the leaders had never been evaluated in their present position, and that the other 82 percent received feedback that was late, ambiguous, and unrelated to the promotion of professional learning. This finding is not a reflection of sour grapes due to poor evaluations. On the contrary, as is the case with teacher evaluations, the overwhelming majority of administrator evaluations are positive. But if assessment is designed to promote learning, then it must convey in unequivocal terms that the person being assessed needs improvement. In the context of education, from kindergarten to the superintendent's office, those words—"needs improvement"—are more likely to start an argument based on a caustic judgment than they are to ignite professional learning. But if formative assessment is, as Popham advocates, a process and not an event, if its purpose is learning and not judgment, then we can accept that "needs improvement" is part of the human condition. It is not a frailty, but an essential element of learning. The Leadership Performance Matrix is available as an open-source document.

Linking Adult Assessments to Student Learning

The evidence in Appendix A makes the essential link by showing that effective assessment of adult learning processes is directly related to improved student learning. The assessment instrument used for the study that led to this finding was the Planning, Implementation, and Monitoring (PIM™) rubric (see Appendix B), now applied to more than 2,000 school plans in the United States and Canada. It includes the following elements: comprehensive needs assessment, inquiry process, specific goals, measurable goals, achievable goals, relevant goals, timely goals, targeted research-based strategies, master plan design, professional development focus, professional development implementation, parental involvement strategies, monitoring plan, monitoring frequency, and evaluation cycle. For each of these elements, the planning, implementation, and monitoring process was assessed on a three-point scale.

For example, the "professional development implementation" domain includes the following range of performance:

• 3—ALL key initiatives described in action steps are supported by specific professional development and targeted research-based strategies. Professional development support is provided for ALL key initiatives in multiple ways. Clear evidence exists that coaching/mentoring is planned schoolwide (examples include peer observations, lesson study, etc.). Consideration of adult learning needs and change processes is clearly evident and reflected in time, strategies, and resources devoted to ALL professional development to sustain growth over time.

- 2—A majority of key initiatives described in action steps are supported by specific professional development and research-based strategies. Professional development support is evident. Examples include time, patient and persistent coaching, mentoring linked with initiatives, and multiple opportunities for training or retraining to support teachers. In a majority of professional development action steps, consideration of adult learning needs and change processes is clearly evident and reflected in time, strategies, and resources (limited initiatives, focused professional development, integrated planning, related support structures, etc.) to sustain growth over time.

- 1—Less than 50 percent of key initiatives described in action steps are supported by specific professional development and research-based strategies. Professional development support is not identified or is not specifically linked to key initiatives described in action steps. Coaching/ mentoring is incidental to the school improvement plan. There is little or no evidence provided of attention to adult learning needs or change processes needed to sustain growth over time.

Throughout the rubric, there is a consistent emphasis on focus, with higher scores related to fewer initiatives. When this rubric was implemented in schools, three important findings emerged. First and most important, increases in student achievement are linked to both absolute scores on the rubric and also to gains in rubric scores from the previous year. Second, the impact on achievement appears to be largest in underperforming schools. That finding does not imply that planning, implementation, and monitoring are unnecessary in high-performing schools, but only that the magnitude of gains is higher when the starting point is lower. Third, and somewhat disturbingly, high scores on the matrix one year are not consistently related to high scores in the next year. Part of this finding may be due to the very high turnover (almost 50 percent) in school leadership in the first 300 schools in which the process was used; this turnover led to inconsistent application of planning and leadership practices. It may also

be due to the fact that the challenges of initiative fatigue and program proliferation are inherent in educational systems, and maintaining high levels
of professional learning requires consistent and focused effort for teachers
and leadership teams.

When the assessments of teachers, leaders, and learning teams are all
aligned to support student learning, great things happen. Not only does
student achievement improve, but the valuable time of teachers and administrators is focused in the right places at the right time. The messages at
every level of the system are consistent, and the feedback, from the classroom to the board room, is constructive and clear. In the final chapter, we
consider a case study of high-impact learning in action.

12

High-Impact Learning in Action

This chapter tells the story of a school leadership team that took on the challenge of high-impact learning. They are neither superstars nor martyrs, and the challenges that they faced were significant but not unusual. Their story represents a composite of observations of many schools, and it is designed to illustrate the challenges and rewards of teachers and leaders who became fully engaged and completely focused on high-impact learning.

The Inheritance

Bernice Johnston inherited many things from her predecessor at Monroe School. Settling into her second month as principal, she had a fine office with fresh paint and new furniture. Her administrative assistant was competent and reasonably courteous. The school itself appeared to be orderly and safe, and the physical facilities were well maintained. Bernice also inherited a staff that was demoralized and unfocused, and a professional development calendar that was crammed with disjointed workshops.

The staff was surprised when Bernice attended the first mandatory after-school workshop, as neither her predecessor nor other building administrators had attended in the past. The meeting was held in the cafeteria, with teachers seated at tables with benches and no backs. The room was stifling, and the teachers, some of whom had been at the school since 6:30 a.m., were exhausted. They were used to the routine, however—two and a half hours of PowerPoint slides, punctuated by a break and a few table discussions. When the meeting adjourned at 5 p.m., Bernice thanked the staff and said, "I think you might have some ideas of how we could do professional learning differently this year. I'd appreciate it if you'd share those with me in the next few days."

Deluged by Details

With that, she headed back to her office. Since her arrival at the school just two weeks before the beginning of the school year, she had been confronted by a series of issues that demanded her immediate attention. Two teachers took positions with other school systems during the summer, and their replacements had not yet been hired. A leak in the roof of the gymnasium had damaged the floor of the basketball court. The master schedule program had generally worked well, but several parents had called to ask how their children could be accumulating sufficient credits when they had two study halls, and several other parents complained that their children were forced to choose between advanced placement classes and the fourth year of world language classes, both of which were scheduled for the same time slot.

Bernice regarded herself as an excellent time manager, and she had been a disciplined creator of daily prioritized task lists since her college days. She had purchased a new planner for the new school year, moving from her previous leather cover to one made of completely recycled materials. Each day she meticulously checked things off the list or moved them forward to a future date. She enjoyed a feeling of completion, certain that nothing was slipping through the cracks.

But after only a few weeks at Monroe, she noticed that many things *were* slipping. Not only was her task list becoming unmanageable, taking several pages in her planner, but a growing stack of documents on her desk remained unread. Worst of all, she knew that although instructional leadership was her primary responsibility, she had devoted scant attention to teaching and learning. The district strategic plan and school improvement plan were in binders on the shelf, but other priorities had prevented her from giving them more than a cursory glance. She had met with the staff as a whole and in several small groups, but had had little one-to-one contact with anyone except the school representative of the teacher's association. The relationship with the union appeared to be satisfactory, with no grievances in the past year. But Bernice also noticed a wariness and a weariness about the faculty, particularly during the workshop. They simply didn't seem to be very happy or engaged, and if that were the case in the second month of the school year, what was it going to be like in the ninth month?

"See Me"

It was nearly 8:00 p.m. when Bernice finished her task list for the next day, emptied her voicemail box, and decided to take one more look at her e-mail. A one-line message from the chief academic officer, Vernon Jackson, had a time stamp of 7:55 p.m. Apparently Bernice was not the only administrator working late. The message simply said "See me." Because the message seemed urgent, Bernice called Dr. Jackson's cell phone, which he immediately answered in his usual businesslike tone. "I saw your message," began Bernice.

"We have a problem," Dr. Jackson interrupted.

"What's wrong?" Bernice asked, wondering if there had been an issue with a student, parent, or faculty member that she had missed.

"Last spring's student achievement data was just released, and Monroe is down again. I'd like to know what you intend to do about it," said Jackson bluntly.

"I haven't even seen the data, and the school year has already started." Bernice was not used to being put on the defensive. She was a capable and confident leader. She knew that Monroe had some achievement challenges, but it was not nearly as bad as some other schools in the district.

"You'll get the data in the morning," Jackson concluded. "And I'll need to see your action plan within two weeks. Based on what I've seen of your 9th and 10th grade results, you've got a train wreck coming in the next year or two. And I don't know if you've noticed, but your faculty has kept peace with parents by putting a lot of kids on the honor roll who are not close to meeting our academic standards. That's what they did to make your predecessor happy, but I hope that is not what you have in mind. Have a good evening."

The next call Bernice made was to the teachers' association representative for Monroe. "I'm so sorry to bother you at home, but something has come up. Could we have coffee first thing tomorrow morning?" She started compiling a list of other people she needed to listen to. Her assistant principal and academic dean were both new to the building, and they had also been inundated by a steady stream of daily crises—scheduling, discipline, hallway monitoring, and substitute teacher coverage. "We need to get refocused," Bernice thought, as she turned the light out in her office.

Surveying the Landscape

James Humphrey was not only Monroe's teacher's association representative; he was also a past president of the association for the entire district. A 28-year veteran social studies teacher, he was liked by his peers and appeared to have a good relationship with his students. He approached Bernice somewhat stiffly and asked, "What can I do for you, Ms. Johnston?"

"I keep asking you to call me Bernice, and I hope you will. I really need your help." She explained the previous evening's call, the impending report of student results, and asked what James knew about it.

"It's not very surprising," Humphrey replied. "For the last several years we've heard the message loud and clear to keep our heads down, don't upset parents or kids, and stay off the radar screen of the head shed—I mean, the superintendent's office—and that's what we've been doing. We show up to those ridiculous workshops that you've got scheduled and try to avoid making trouble."

"OK," said Bernice hesitantly. "Please tell me more. You know, the workshops were scheduled last year."

"Look," James replied. "It's always been that way. It's like I teach my students in world history about the old Soviet Union. The workers would say, 'We pretend to work, and the government pretends to pay us.'"

"C'mon," Bernice interrupted. "It's not exactly a gulag here."

"You were in the cafeteria with us. You saw the two-and-a-half-hour punishment we endured. Couldn't we at least have chairs with backs on them?"

After a long pause, Bernice replied, "We're going to do a lot better than that. Starting today, every one of those workshops is canceled, and I'm going to need your help and the help of our best people to completely redesign professional learning for this year. I'm open to anything—different times, different places, and different formats. Frankly, I think we have a lot to learn from each other, and I'm willing to pull my share of the professional development load. Actually, I sort of like doing that, and I especially like doing it when my colleagues are working together with me to plan and execute it. But right now, I'd better go and greet our students. Thanks for the time."

From Frazzled to Focused

Bernice quickly assembled a Learning Task Force that included not only her administrators and Mr. Humphrey but also a representation of different departments and a wide range of experience levels, from nontenured teachers with fewer than 5 years of service to veterans with more than 30 years. They started by conducting an "initiative inventory," listing everything that was on the school's agenda, from their school plan to the staff development calendar to occasional policy memoranda to a number of casually created, spontaneous initiatives, typically the result of the principal's attendance at a recent conference. They found, to their dismay, 77 different initiatives, all of which had been labeled as a priority.

The team then agreed on two simple criteria to evaluate each of the 77 pending initiatives. The first question was "Are we really using it?" The second question was "Is there strong evidence that it is directly related to improving student performance?" By the end of their first meeting, the team had winnowed the list of 77 items to only 15 that met both criteria. "That's still too many," Bernice insisted, and after some strong discussion, the group was able to narrow their focus to six critical areas: literacy in every class, on-time attendance, differentiated feedback intervals, failure prevention, homework completion, and formative assessment.

"Great work!" Bernice said, with clear appreciation and enthusiasm. "We've taken the first step to get Monroe back on track. For our next meeting, I'd like to ask you to come prepared to address two questions for each of our six priorities. What will teachers do this month, this quarter, and this semester, to address each of these six priorities? What do I and my administrative team need to do in order to support teachers in each of these priorities?"

After the meeting, the assistant principal and the academic dean made some very uncomfortable calls to workshop presenters whose engagements were canceled and vendors whose programs were being terminated. The vendors seemed unfazed by the fact that some of the programs, for which the school had been paying monthly license fees, had not been used for more than a year. "If you are not implementing our program with fidelity," they protested, "that's not our fault." Despite threats that the district central office would be notified of these poor decisions, the dean and assistant principal were polite and firm. Monroe was going to be a focused school.

The New Reality

By the end of the next meeting of the Learning Task Force, the six priorities of the school took on greater clarity, and the team was ready to communicate its new direction to the entire faculty. When Bernice first announced all the initiatives, programs, and workshops that had been taken off the table, the crowd cheered—the first genuine ovation they had offered to any administrator at any level for a very long time. Then several task force members briefly addressed their vision for each of the six priorities, including the support that they needed from each classroom teacher and the specific ways in which the school administration would support teachers.

It soon became apparent that professional development had not been canceled but was going to be radically changed. It would be in the morning rather than the afternoon; almost all of the facilitators would be from the teaching and administrative staff, not from outside; and each workshop would be linked to the student achievement results contained in the six priorities. Not everyone appreciated these changes, particularly when they learned that the cancellations included not only the dreadful after-school workshops but also some of their favorite activities. The team remained unified and supportive, however, and when James Humphrey said, "We may not all agree about this, but let's give this team the benefit of the doubt," the dissenters seemed to be willing to do so, or at least to refrain from active opposition.

Bernice concluded the meeting by noting, "This task force can't do this alone. With the money we are saving from things we have canceled, I'm able to pay stipends to those of you willing to engage in action research. We'll have a voluntary action research workshop during each of the three lunch periods on Thursday and Friday, so if you'd like to brown-bag it, I'll explain more about how that will work. Essentially, we'll ask you to identify a research question that directly supports one of our six priorities that you are willing to undertake with your students. That process will involve collecting data not only on student performance, but also on the specific teaching strategies you undertook. I think we can all learn from each other this year."

The Hot Seat

It had been a week since Bernice received the "See me" e-mail from the chief academic officer. She had seven days to submit her action plan, and in a district that had a history of using long and complex planning documents, she was a little hesitant to offer her two-page action plan. It simply had three columns, with the first displaying one of the six priorities, the second column containing specific teaching strategies, and the third column identifying specific areas of leadership support. She thought that it might be wise to speak to Dr. Jackson about it before the due date.

"Thanks for calling," he said. "You were on my list to call anyway. Did you know that Dr. Beckel, the workshop presenter you terminated, is the brother-in-law of Mrs. Beckel who is on our school board? She just gave me an earful."

"Sorry," replied Bernice. "I didn't know that. But I still think it was the right decision to make."

"I'll back you up on it," Jackson continued. "Now you're not the only one on the hot seat. Unhappy board members can make life very difficult for the superintendent and for me. I need you to make this work."

"We're going to do just that. In fact, you might want to drop by some time. I think you'll see that the morale of this faculty has changed in a very significant way in the past few days. I need to earn their trust and follow through on these commitments. But if we can get some short-term wins and have your support, I think you will see that this is going to be a very different school this year."

"How Long Is This Going to Take?"

Toward the end of the first semester, the task force had to deal with some mixed results. The faculty did seem happier, and some very preliminary success stories told of teachers' use of creative strategies for improving student performance. It was particularly reaffirming to see teachers like James Humphrey take a lead in introducing explicit literacy instruction into social studies classes. Similar standout performances occurred in music, art, and physical education—departments that administrators had ignored for years. But for the most part, these seemed to be islands of excellence and not a schoolwide reform. The dean's report of first-quarter grades was not encouraging either, with virtually no change in student performance compared with the first quarter of the previous year. Jean Dennison, 24 years old and in her second year of teaching, had been an enthusiastic participant in the work but seemed devastated by the lack of progress. "We've been doing this for three months and don't have much to show for it," she complained. "How long is this going to take?"

The room was quiet as everyone waited for Bernice to respond. "I'll tell you the truth. If the question is how long the process of improving teaching and learning will take, then the answer is, the rest of your career. But if the question is how long it will take us to show results from our work, then the answer is that every month we need to have performance data that demonstrate the impact of our work. I know that you were disappointed by the dean's report on first-quarter grade-point averages, but that's only a small piece of the picture. Let's go back to our priorities and think of other data we can gather to share with the faculty in the next few days before winter break starts. Jeremy, could you nail down the number of formative assessments that have been administered so far? Ask people just two questions: how many in the first semester of last year, and how many so far in the first semester of this year." She continued around the room, with each task force member agreeing to gather just one indicator number for each of the priorities.

There is no ending to this story. It represents not a "happily ever after" fable, but a realistic depiction of the challenges and rewards that happen during the first weeks and months of a commitment to high-impact learning. I have worked with educational systems that have consistently applied these principles for more than a decade. They are still engaging in action research, performance assessment for teachers and leaders, and narrowing the focus of their planning and monitoring. Each year they have to weed the garden of excess initiatives, and in some cases, teachers and leaders have expressed frustration that it feels as if they are starting over. In a series of interviews I conducted with principals who had achieved sustained success in challenging school environments, the last interview question was this: "What do you know now that you wish you had known when you started?" Perhaps I was hoping for sage words of encouragement to soothe the burden for new leaders. That is not, however, what I heard. In fact, the most frequent response was "I wish I knew that it never got easier."

When I asked the respondents to explain this unexpected answer, they said that they originally thought that if they delayed change, then the next year people would like it more. In truth, these successful leaders told me, there are simply always going to be elements of dissatisfaction. Some students and parents are wedded to a schedule, so late starts for professional learning are a significant inconvenience for them. Some teachers and administrators are deeply committed to previous practices, so asking for changes—particularly in assessment and grading—causes some major push-back. Even people who should be supportive, such as some fellow administrators and supervisors, would sometimes give contradictory messages, as if they cared more about popularity than effectiveness.

High-impact learning is not about creating a life of efficiency and ease for teachers and leaders. It is about undertaking the challenge of professional work with deep meaning and lifelong impact. The journey is neither easy nor popular, but the rewards of helping colleagues and students improve their learning environment will be incomparable. I invite you to take the next step on the journey.

APPENDIX A

Results of a Study of School Planning, Implementation, and Monitoring

The charts in this appendix represent the relationship between **student achievement in reading and math** and **school performance on the dimensions of planning, implementation, and monitoring.** For each chart, the vertical axis shows percentage gains in student achievement, the grade level, and subject. The horizontal axis represents the rubric score—1, 2, or 3. The details describing each of those ratings are shown in Appendix B.

The data were gathered from schools in the United States and Canada from 2005 to 2008 and are based on independent analyses of school planning, implementation, and monitoring processes. Information on student achievement was provided by the school systems or secured from publicly available sources, such as the district or state Web sites.

As with any analysis of correlation, we are not claiming that the district actions in planning, implementation, and monitoring were the exclusive causes of changes in student achievement. Nevertheless, the associations are clear and consistent, suggesting that when teachers and school leaders collaborate to achieve the highest ratings in planning, implementation, and monitoring, then they also are more likely to achieve gains in student results in reading and math.

The charts are arranged by subject, beginning with reading and language arts, and followed by mathematics.

FIGURE A.1
Timely Goals and Reading Achievement in 8th Grade

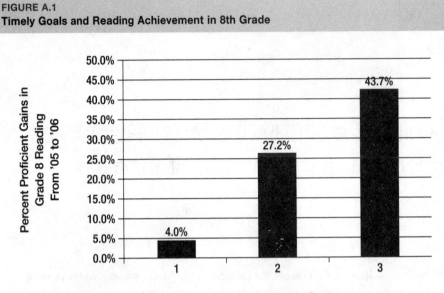

FIGURE A.2
Comprehensive Needs Assessment and Reading Achievement in 4th Grade

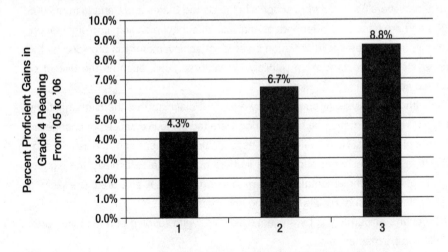

FIGURE A.3
Comprehensive Needs Assessment and Reading Achievement in 3rd Grade

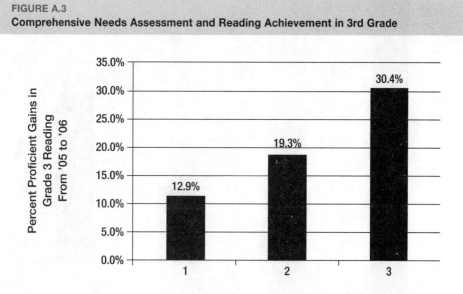

Score on Comprehensive Needs Assessment

FIGURE A.4
Professional Development Focus and Reading Achievement in 11th Grade

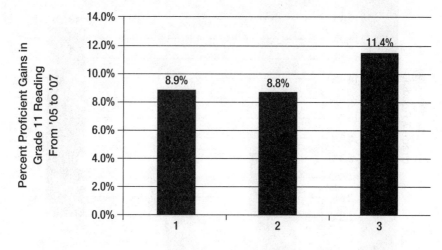

Score on Professional Development Focus

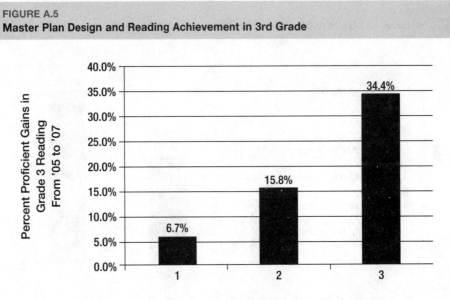

FIGURE A.5
Master Plan Design and Reading Achievement in 3rd Grade

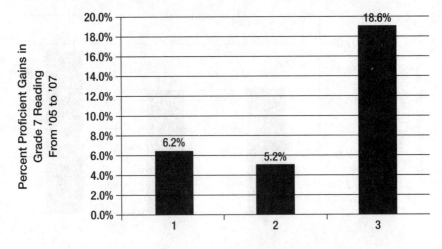

FIGURE A.6
Master Plan Design and Reading Achievement in 7th Grade

FIGURE A.7
Professional Development Gaps and Language Achievement in 7th Grade

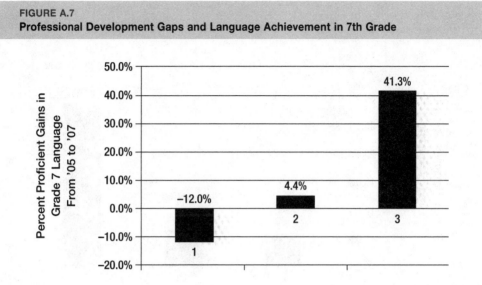

Score on Professional Development Gaps

FIGURE A.8
Professional Development Gaps and Reading Achievement in 3rd Grade

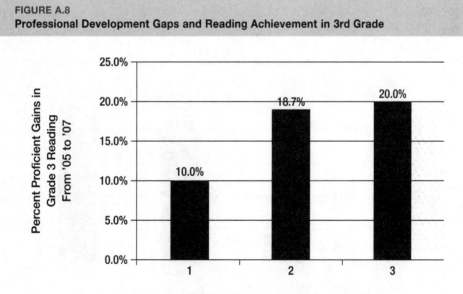

Score on Professional Development Gaps

FIGURE A.9
Professional Development Gaps and Reading Achievement in 7th Grade

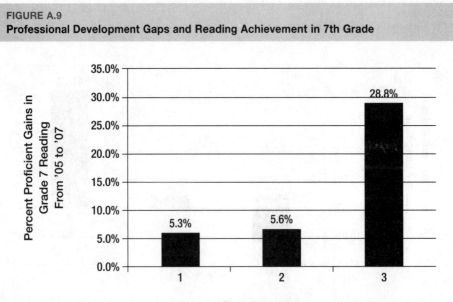

Score on Professional Development Gaps

FIGURE A.10
Specific Goals and Reading Achievement in 3rd Grade

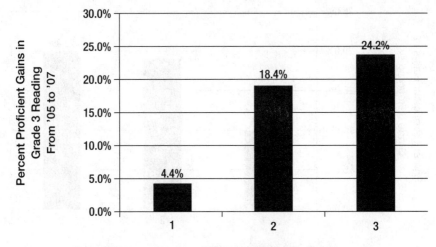

Score on Specific Goals

FIGURE A.11
Measurable Goals and Reading Achievement in 3rd Grade

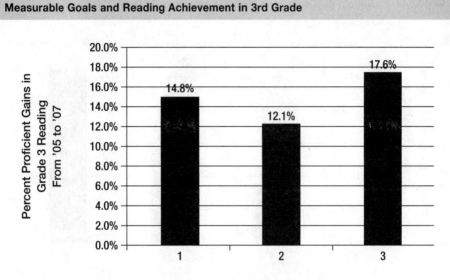

Score on Measurable Goals

FIGURE A.12
Relevant Goals and Reading Achievement in 3rd Grade

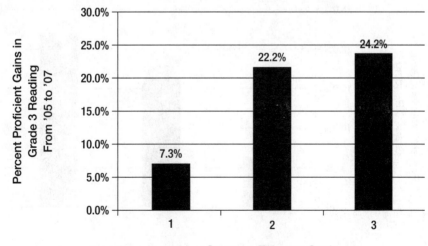

Score on Relevant Goals

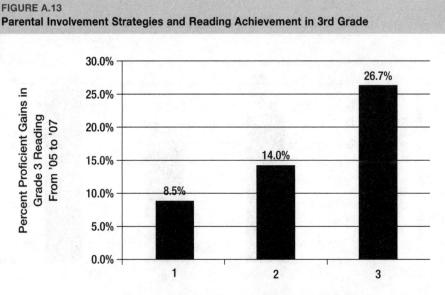

FIGURE A.13
Parental Involvement Strategies and Reading Achievement in 3rd Grade

Score on Parental Involvement Strategies

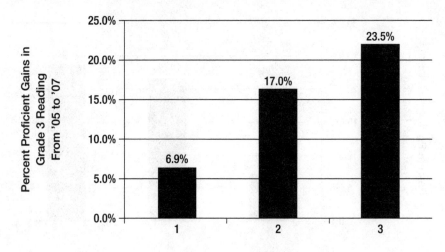

FIGURE A.14
Monitoring Frequency and Reading Achievement in 3rd Grade

Score on Monitoring Frequency

FIGURE A.15
Measurable Goals and Reading Achievement in 4th Grade

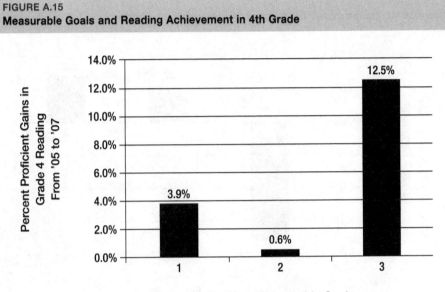

Score on Measurable Goals

FIGURE A.16
Measurable Goals and Language Achievement in 7th Grade

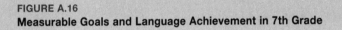

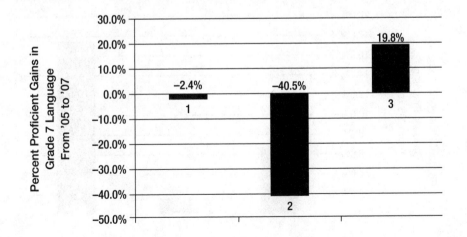

Score on Measurable Goals

FIGURE A.17
Monitoring Frequency and Language Achievement in 7th Grade

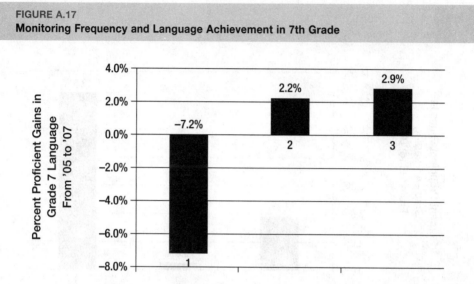

Score on Monitoring Frequency

FIGURE A.18
Monitoring Plan and Reading Achievement in 4th Grade

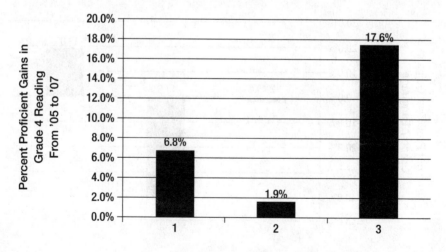

Score on Monitoring Plan

FIGURE A.19
Targeted Research-Based Strategies and Reading Achievement in 5th Grade

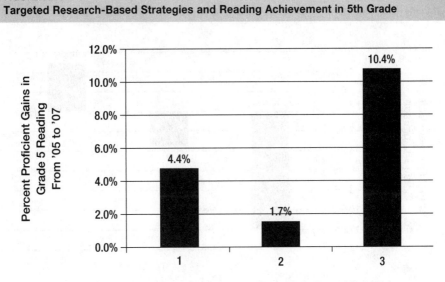

Score on Targeted Research-Based Strategies

FIGURE A.20
Specific Goals and Reading Achievement in 3rd Grade

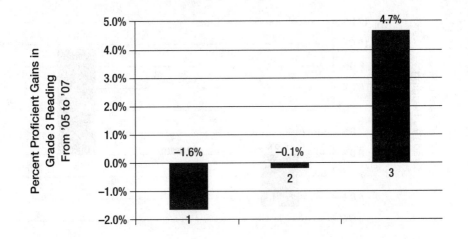

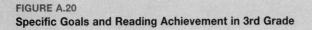

Score on Specific Goals

FIGURE A.21
Specific Goals and Language Achievement in 7th Grade

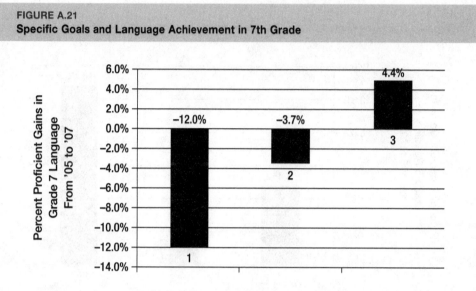

Score on Specific Goals

FIGURE A.22
Professional Development Gaps and Reading Achievement in 10th Grade

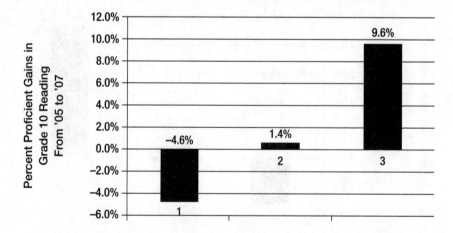

Score on Professional Development Gaps

FIGURE A.23
Comprehensive Needs and Language Achievement in 4th Grade

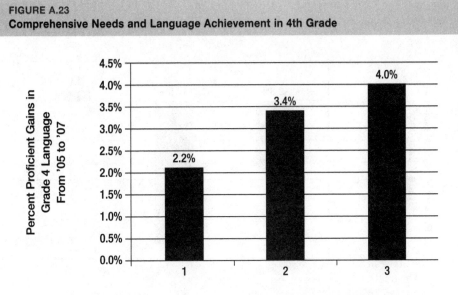

FIGURE A.24
Professional Development Strategies and Reading Achievement in 10th Grade

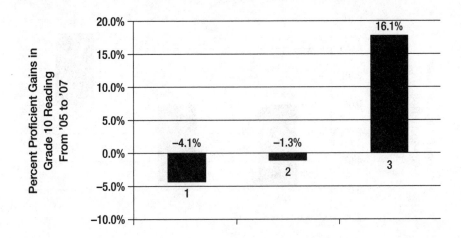

FIGURE A.25
Achievable Goals and Language Achievement in 7th Grade

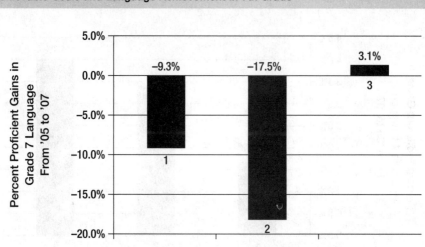

Score on Achievable Goals

FIGURE A.26
Achievable Goals and Reading Achievement in 10th Grade

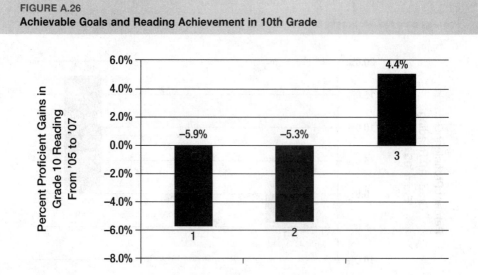

Score on Achievable Goals

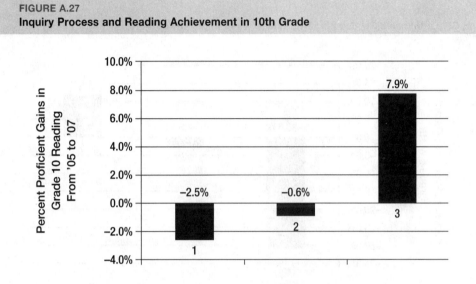

FIGURE A.27
Inquiry Process and Reading Achievement in 10th Grade

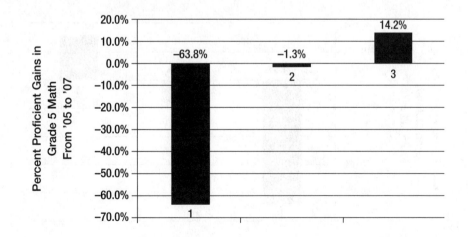

FIGURE A.28
Specific Goals and Math Achievement in 5th Grade

FIGURE A.29
Comprehensive Needs and Math Achievement in 5th Grade

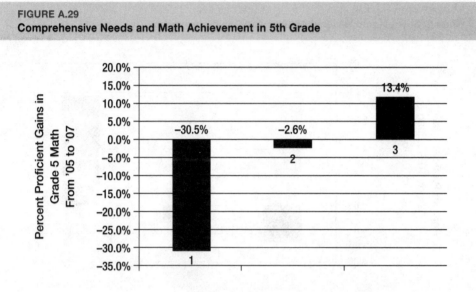

Score on Comprehensive Needs

FIGURE A.30
Inquiry Process and Math Achievement in 5th Grade

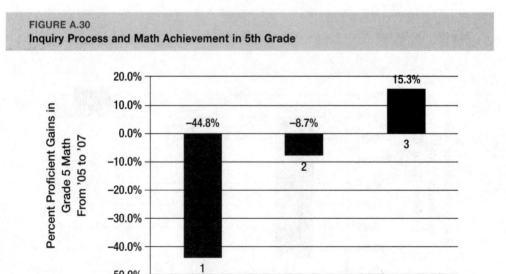

Score on Inquiry Process

FIGURE A.31
Professional Development Gaps and Math Achievement in 4th Grade

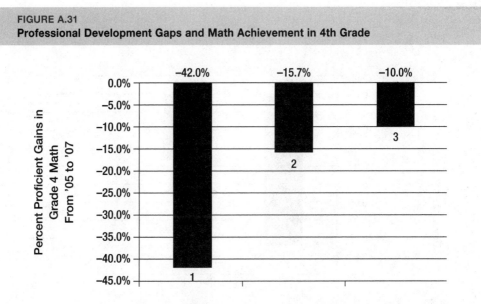

Score on Professional Development Gaps

FIGURE A.32
Achievable Goals and Math Achievement in 4th Grade

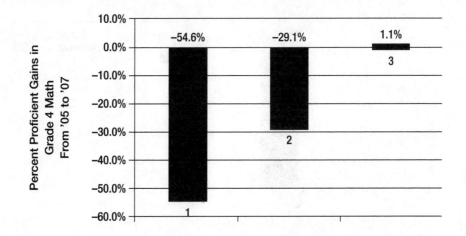

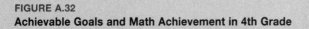

Score on Achievable Goals

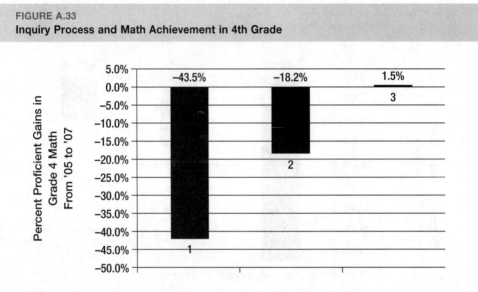

FIGURE A.33
Inquiry Process and Math Achievement in 4th Grade

Percent Proficient Gains in Grade 4 Math From '05 to '07

−43.5%   −18.2%   1.5%

Score on Inquiry Process

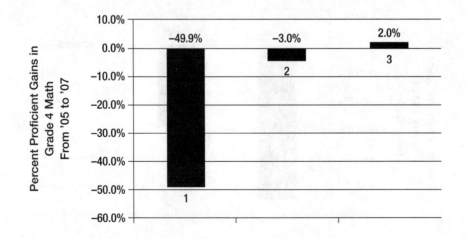

FIGURE A.34
Relevant Goals and Math Achievement in 4th Grade

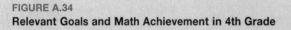

Percent Proficient Gains in Grade 4 Math From '05 to '07

−49.9%   −3.0%   2.0%

Score on Relevant Goals

FIGURE A.35
Relevant Goals and Math Achievement in 5th Grade

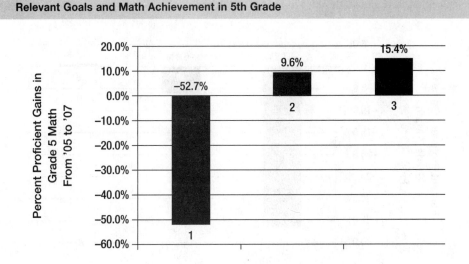

Score on Relevant Goals

FIGURE A.36
Achievable Goals and Math Achievement in 5th Grade

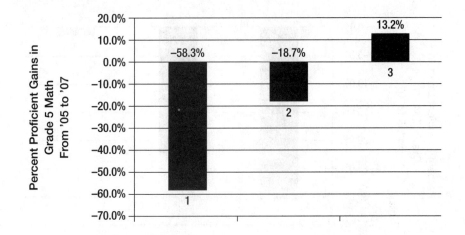

Score on Achievable Goals

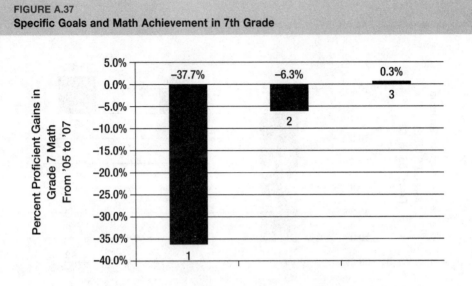

FIGURE A.37
Specific Goals and Math Achievement in 7th Grade

Score on Specific Goals

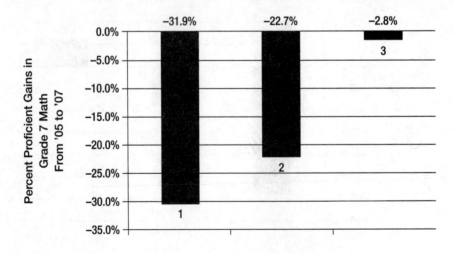

FIGURE A.38
Achievable Goals and Math Achievement in 7th Grade

Score on Achievable Goals

FIGURE A.39
Professional Development Gaps and Math Achievement in 7th Grade

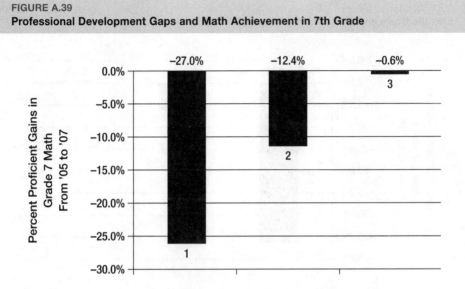

Score on Professional Development Gaps

FIGURE A.40
Inquiry Process and Math Achievement in 7th Grade

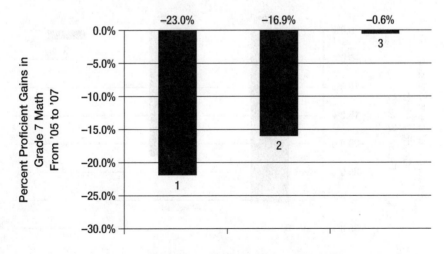

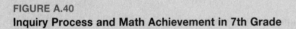

Score on Inquiry Process

FIGURE A.41
Specific Goals and Math Achievement in 7th Grade

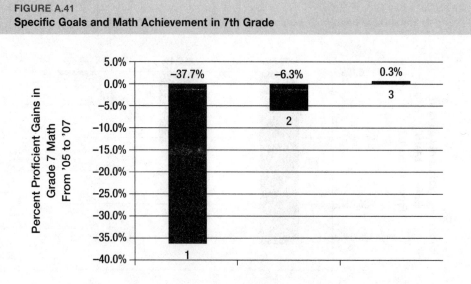

Score on Specific Goals

FIGURE A.42
Achievable Goals and Math Achievement in 7th Grade

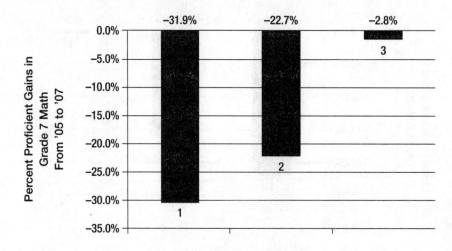

Score on Achievable Goals

FIGURE A.43
Timely Goals and Math Achievement in 7th Grade

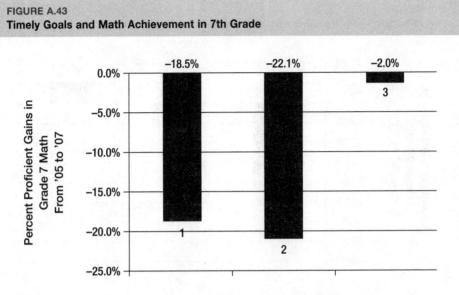

Score on Timely Goals

FIGURE A.44
Professional Development Goals and Math Achievement in 7th Grade

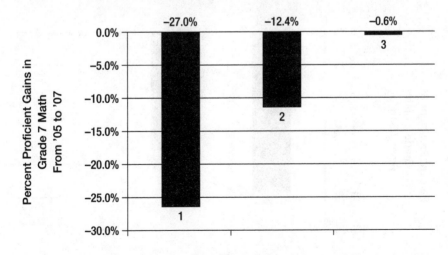

Score on Professional Development Goals

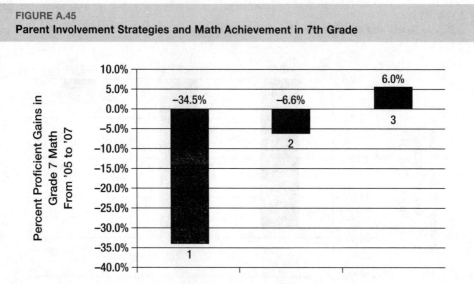

FIGURE A.45
Parent Involvement Strategies and Math Achievement in 7th Grade

Score on Parent Involvement Strategies

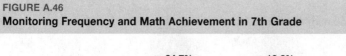

FIGURE A.46
Monitoring Frequency and Math Achievement in 7th Grade

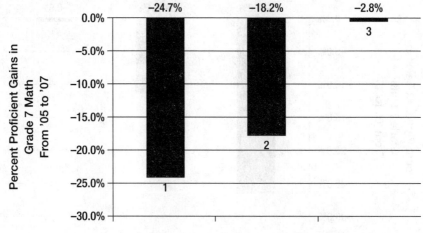

Score on Monitoring Frequency

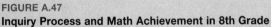

FIGURE A.47
Inquiry Process and Math Achievement in 8th Grade

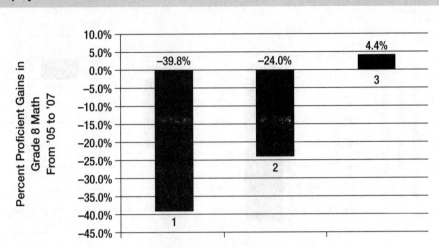

Score on Inquiry Process

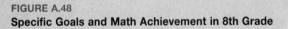

FIGURE A.48
Specific Goals and Math Achievement in 8th Grade

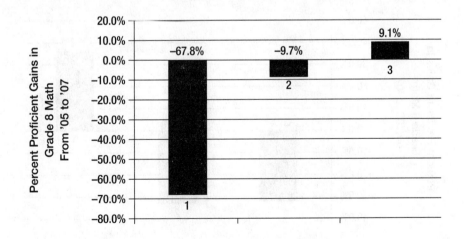

Score on Specific Goals

FIGURE A.49
Achievable Goals and Math Achievement in 8th Grade

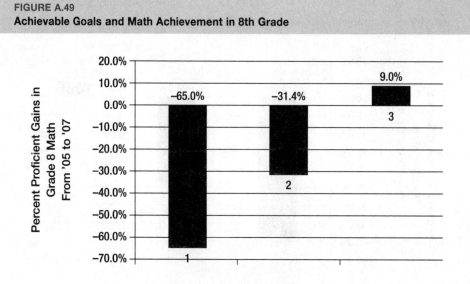

Score on Achievable Goals

FIGURE A.50
Timely Goals and Math Achievement in 8th Grade

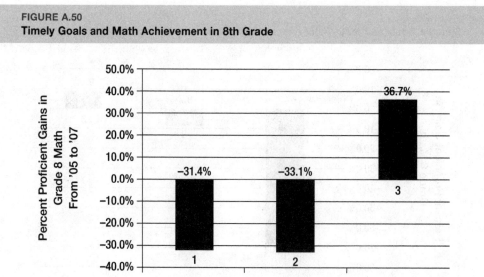

Score on Timely Goals

FIGURE A.51
Monitoring Plan and Math Achievement in 8th Grade

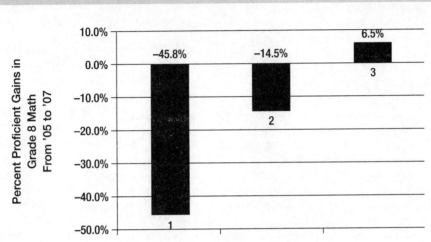

Score on Monitoring Plan

FIGURE A.52
Monitoring Parental Involvement Strategies and Science Achievement in 4th Grade

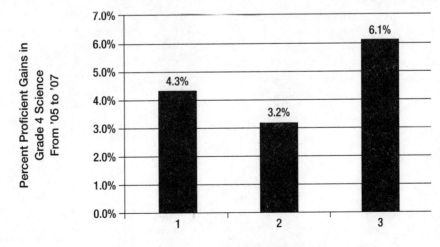

Score on Parental Involvement

APPENDIX B

Planning, Implementation, and Monitoring (PIM™) Rubric

SECTION A: PLANNING

Comprehensive Needs Assessment

3 (In addition to 2)	2	1
a) The plan provides evidence of the school's leadership (decisions regarding use of time, assignment of staff, allocation of resources, collaboration, feedback, etc.) to support the school's learning processes. b) Challenges (areas in need of improvement) are specified in student achievement, teaching, and leadership practices. c) Student achievement data explicitly describes common formative assessments or student work samples. d) The majority of identified needs are based on both quantitative and qualitative data.	a) The plan provides evidence of the school's learning effectiveness (for instance, student subgroup and subscale achievement data, teaching practices, classroom and department trends and/or patterns). b) Challenges in both student achievement and adult practices (actions of educators) are specific enough to guide and facilitate other components of the school's improvement plan. c) Student achievement data includes evidence of school-level data (such as end-of-course assessments, diagnostic assessments, performance assessments, classroom management, time on task) to support district or state assessment data. d) At least one identified need is based on both quantitative and qualitative data.	a) The school has yet to perform a comprehensive analysis of the school's learning (instructional) effectiveness. b) Challenges presented are limited to student achievement or adult practices, rather than both. It is difficult to determine what should change at the school, because the data presented is insufficient. c) Identified district-level achievement needs are rarely supported with specific school-based data. d) The identified needs may be based on quantitative or qualitative data, rather than both.

Inquiry Process

3 (In addition to 2)	2	1
a) The school identifies prioritized cause-and-effect relationships from the comprehensive needs assessment. b) The school plan focuses on both leadership and learning effectiveness to identify 6 or fewer priorities in ALL goal areas that are linked to the causes of current problems and successes in student achievement. Leadership examples include school scheduling, grouping, meetings, monitoring, and feedback. Examples of learning effectiveness are teaching practices such as high-yield instructional strategies, grouping, and use of assessments. c) All causes identified are factors within the direct control of educators and ALL are school-based issues (such as professional practices of teachers and leaders, particularly with regard to teaching strategies, assessment practices, feedback techniques, and curriculum).	a) The school uses the comprehensive needs assessment to narrow the areas of focus and identify some cause-and-effect relationships. b) The school plan focuses on learning effectiveness to identify priorities (6 or fewer) in at least one goal area that are linked to the causes of current problems and successes in student achievement delineated in the plan. c) The majority of causes identified are factors within the direct control of educators and ALL are school-based issues (such as professional practices of teachers and leaders, particularly with regard to teaching strategies, assessment practices, feedback techniques, and curriculum).	a) The plan tends to address broad content-area improvements without identifying the links between student needs and the actions of educators to current problems and successes in student achievement. b) Either the school identifies some causes of current problems and successes unrelated to instructional best practices or identifies so many causes that establishing a clear focus is unlikely. c) Causes tend to be demographic or pertain to individual students and their families rather than the actions of educators. There is little evidence that root causes have been identified that result in achievement shortfalls.

SMART GOALS

Specific Goals

3 (In addition to 2)	2	1
a) ALL school improvement plan goals are aligned to academic content standards and related subskills within the standards. b) ALL school improvement plan goals are specific to individual grade levels and groups of students.	a) One or more school improvement goals within the plan are aligned to academic content standards and related subskills within the standards. b) One or more school improvement goals within the plan are specific to students (related to both individual grade and group levels).	a) School improvement goals tend to address general content areas and do not address standards and related subskills. b) School improvement goals tend to address general student needs and do not relate to specific grade levels or to specific groups of students.

Measurable Goals

3 (In addition to 2)	2	1
a) ALL goals within the school improvement plan are measurable. b) The school improvement plan establishes clear baseline data for ALL of its goals.	a) The majority of school improvement goals are measurable (using quantifiable measures such as percentages or other numeric systems). b) The majority of school improvement goals identify baseline data to measure progress toward achieving the goals.	a) Less than 50 percent of school improvement goals are measurable. b) Less than 50 percent of school improvement goals identify the baseline data needed to measure progress toward goal attainment.

Achievable Goals

3 (In addition to 2)	2	1
a) ALL goals are sufficiently challenging to close learning gaps for targeted groups or subskills in three to five years. b) ALL goals chosen are of sufficient significance that attaining them will contribute, in important ways, to the school's overall record of student achievement (see minimal growth targets below).	a) The majority of school improvement goals are challenging and attainable for targeted groups or subskills and will close achievement gaps within the next three to five years (that is, the percentage gains are significant enough to eliminate the achievement gap within this time period). b) Attainment of these goals will narrow achievement gaps within the school (see minimal growth targets below).	a) Less than 50 percent of school improvement goals are sufficiently challenging. As a result, attaining them will make little difference to the school's overall level of student achievement. b) Attainment of these goals is unlikely to narrow achievement gaps within the school (see minimal growth targets below).

Minimal Growth from Baseline to Close Gaps: First Quartile ≥ 20%; 2nd Quartile ≥ 12%; 3rd Quartile ≥ 7%; Highest Quartile ≥ 4%

Relevant Goals

3 (In addition to 2)	2	1
a) ALL goals represent urgent, critical needs within the school and align with priorities established through the inquiry process.	a) The majority of school improvement goals align with priorities established through the inquiry process.	a) Less than 50 percent of school improvement goals align with priorities established through the inquiry process.

Timely Goals

3 (In addition to 2)	2	1
a) ALL of the goals within the school improvement plan identify specific dates (season, month, or day) for assessment, data collection, and analysis.	a) The majority of school improvement goals identify specific dates (season, month, or day) for measurement of the goals.	a) Less than 50 percent of school improvement goals identify specific dates (season, month, or day) for measurement of the goals.

SECTION B: IMPLEMENTATION

Targeted Research-Based Strategies

3 (In addition to 2)	2	1
a) ALL of the instructional strategies outlined are grounded in sound research for standards-based practices. Evidence demonstrates how supporting strategies will improve achievement. b) ALL schoolwide programs or instructional strategies (such as NCLB research-based programs, collaborative scoring, dual-block algebra, looping, tailored summer school) specify the student group that needs the service.	a) A majority of the instructional strategies are informed by the research on effective classroom and school practices (such as Marzano's *Art and Science of Teaching* and works by other educational researchers). b) A majority of schoolwide instructional programs or strategies (such as NCLB research-based programs, collaborative scoring, dual-block algebra, looping, tailored summer school) specify the student group that needs the service.	a) Less than 50 percent of the instructional strategies are informed by research. Many simply list programs or activities rather than instructional strategies. b) Less than 50 percent of instructional strategies specified are informed by the research on effective classroom and school practices, or less than 50 percent of strategies specify the student group in need of the strategy or service.

Master Plan Design

3 (In addition to 2)	2	1
a) ALL action steps provide clear guidance for planning, implementation, and monitoring (how, when, in what settings, by whom, to what degree, and why the action will be taken). The plan is sufficiently clear so anyone in the school can understand what is required in order to ensure effective implementation.	a) A majority of action steps provide clear guidance for planning, implementation, and monitoring (how, when, in what settings, by whom, to what degree, and why the action will be taken).	a) Less than 50 percent of action steps are purposeful in terms of timeline, sequence, adult learning needs, and implementation logistics, such as alignment, application, and fidelity.

3 (In addition to 2)	2	1
b) ALL of the action steps have a designated and appropriate person responsible for implementation, rather than several administrators or staff members. c) ALL of the action steps and timelines for each objective and strategy are coordinated with each other. d) ALL major initiatives include midcourse corrections that describe capacity for rapid team responses and support when adjustments are warranted. e) ALL action steps represent *only* planned improvements in school practice. f) The master plan is a concise blueprint with no more than 10 action steps for *each* goal.	b) A majority of action steps have a designated and appropriate person or team responsible for implementation, rather than several administrators or list of staff members without clear responsibility and ownership. c) A majority of action steps and timelines for goals and strategies are coordinated with each other. d) At least one midcourse correction describes capacity for rapid team responses and support when adjustments are warranted (evidence of improvement cycles and plan-do-study-act cycles, for instance). e) Action steps generally describe planned improvements that will change school practices. f) The master plan is a concise blueprint with no more than 10 steps for at least one goal area.	b) Less than 50 percent of the action steps have designated an appropriate person responsible for implementation. c) Less than 50 percent of the action steps and timelines for goals and strategies are coordinated with each other. d) There is no evidence of midcourse corrections planned within the design. e) Action steps generally describe activities and events that represent current and traditional actions rather than planned improvements in practice. f) There are so many action steps specified that implementation will be unlikely.

Professional Development Focus

3 (In addition to 2)	2	1
a) The professional development focus is limited to not more than three professional development initiatives that will impact student achievement—initiatives that are well aligned with school and district goals. b) ALL professional development activities maintain a school-based focus. Teachers learn new instructional strategies to be applied in classrooms schoolwide, and administrators learn how to supervise and evaluate teachers in light of these new strategies.	a) The professional development focus includes not more than five professional development initiatives that will impact student achievement—initiatives that are aligned with school and district goals. b) A majority of professional development activities maintain a school-based focus. Teachers learn new instructional strategies to be applied in their classrooms, and administrators learn how to supervise and evaluate teachers in light of these new strategies.	a) The professional development plan lacks focus. The plan tends to be too extensive, with multiple and/or unrelated professional development strategies. b) Few of the professional development activities maintain a school-based focus. The plan typically describes instructional strategies with little reference to the professional development needed by teachers to implement these strategies.

Professional Development Implementation

3 (In addition to 2)	2	1
a) ALL key initiatives described in action steps are supported by specific professional development and targeted research-based strategies.	a) A majority of key initiatives described in action steps are supported by specific professional development and research-based strategies.	a) Less than 50 percent of key initiatives described in action steps are supported by specific professional development and research-based strategies.

3 (In addition to 2)	2	1
b) Professional development support is provided for ALL key initiatives in multiple ways. Clear evidence exists that coaching/mentoring is planned schoolwide (examples include peer observations, lesson study, etc.). c) Consideration of adult learning needs and change processes is clearly evident and reflected in time, strategies, and resources devoted to ALL professional development to sustain growth over time.	b) Professional development support is evident. Examples include time, patient and persistent coaching, mentoring linked with initiatives, and multiple opportunities for training or retraining to support teachers. c) In a majority of professional development action steps, consideration of adult learning needs and change processes is clearly evident and reflected in time, strategies, and resources (limited initiatives, focused professional development, integrated planning, related support structures, etc.) to sustain growth over time.	b) Professional development support is not identified or is not specifically linked to key initiatives described in action steps. Coaching/mentoring is incidental to the school improvement plan. c) There is little or no evidence provided of attention to adult learning needs or change processes needed to sustain growth over time.

Parental Involvement Strategies

3 (In addition to 2)	2	1
a) Action steps describe empowering ways to include parents in improving student achievement (for example, helping parents learn how to use a nonfiction writing rubric to help students with their writing at home). b) Action steps for ALL goal areas describe parent training and education to enhance involvement in their student's academic achievement. c) Action steps differentiate and describe frequent communications with parents (beyond traditional grading periods) to meet the unique needs of parents (including the use of technology, flexible conference times, and print/phone/conferences in the primary language of the parent).	a) Action steps, within at least one goal area, describe explicitly how the school intends to involve parents to achieve the improvement needed (online student monitoring, participation in curriculum design, methods to support learning at home, etc.). b) Action steps, within at least one goal area, describe parent training and education to enhance involvement in their student's academic achievement. c) Action steps, within at least one goal area, describe how the school will communicate the planned improvements (changes in school practices) to parents.	a) Action steps either omit references to parent involvement or describe nonacademic ways to involve parents (for instance, the percentage of participation in conferences, attendance at school events, newsletters, etc.). b) Action steps do not describe parent training and education. c) Action steps do not describe how the school will communicate the planned improvements (changes in school practices) to parents.

SECTION C: MONITORING

Monitoring Plan

3 (In addition to 2)	2	1
a) The monitoring plan describes explicit data to be monitored, when it will be monitored, and who will be responsible for reporting progress for ALL school improvement goals.	a) The monitoring plan describes explicit data to be monitored, as well as when and who will be responsible for monitoring and reporting progress for a majority of school improvement goals.	a) The monitoring plan fails to describe explicit data to be monitored, when it will be monitored, and who will be responsible for reporting progress for a majority of goals.

3 (In addition to 2)	2	1
b) The monitoring of student achievement assessment data includes a range of assessment data (annual assessments, quarterly benchmarks, monthly probes, and common formative assessments) evident in each goal area. c) The plan includes examples of monitoring improved teaching practices (degree of implementation, percentage of teachers collaborating, number of teachers posting data) in each goal area. d) The monitoring plan distributes monitoring responsibility by assigning responsibility to individual champions for each action step.	b) The monitoring of student achievement assessment data includes a range of assessment data (annual assessments, quarterly benchmarks, monthly probes, and common formative assessments) that are evident throughout the school improvement plan. c) The plan includes at least one example of monitoring of improved teaching practices (degree of implementation, percentage of teachers collaborating, or number of teachers posting data). d) The monitoring plan distributes monitoring responsibility across a range of individuals.	b) The monitoring of student achievement assessment data is limited to annual achievement results. c) No evidence of monitoring of teaching practices is described in the school improvement plan. d) The monitoring plan rarely distributes monitoring responsibility across a range of individuals; it tends to rely on one or two individuals to conduct all of the data collection and analysis.
Monitoring Frequency		
3 (In addition to 2)	**2**	**1**
a) The school improvement plan includes weekly monitoring of student achievement or improvements in teaching practice. b) The timeline lists explicit dates or weeks in which each monitoring activity will occur. c) Monitoring schedules are described that review student performance, teaching practices, and leadership practices.	a) The school improvement plan allows for frequent monitoring (5 to 10 times annually) of student achievement and a related teaching practice. b) The timeline created specifies data collection by the month, term, or specific date. c) Monitoring schedules to review both student performance and some teaching practices.	a) The school improvement plan monitors student achievement four times or fewer annually. b) The timeline created is vague; the timeline does not state specifically which data will be collected at which times. c) Monitoring schedules may exist to review student achievement or teaching practices, rather than both.
Evaluation Cycle		
3 (In addition to 2)	**2**	**1**
a) The evaluation plan is designed to compare planned results with actual outcomes in student performance for ALL goals. b) The evaluation plan is designed to distinguish cause-and-effect variables in describing how lessons learned will be applied to future school improvement plans. c) The evaluation plan is designed explicitly to describe the steps that the school should take to institutionalize successes and eliminate unsuccessful practices.	a) The evaluation plan is designed to compare planned outcomes with actual outcomes in student achievement for at least one goal. b) The evaluation plan is designed to describe how lessons learned will be applied to future school improvement plans. c) The evaluation plan is designed to be transparent in describing how compared results (positive and negative) are communicated to primary stakeholders (families, educators, staff, patrons, partners, and the public).	a) The evaluation plan is not designed to compare planned with actual outcomes. b) The evaluation plan fails to describe how lessons learned will be applied to future school improvement plans. c) The evaluation plan is not designed to describe a process for communicating results.

Source: ©2009 The Leadership and Learning Center. Reprinted with permission.

REFERENCES

Ainsworth, L. (2003a). *Power standards: Identifying the standards that matter the most.* Englewood, CO: Advanced Learning Press.

Ainsworth, L. (2003b). *"Unwrapping" the standards: A simple process to make standards manageable.* Englewood, CO: Advanced Learning Press.

Ainsworth, L., & Viegut, D. (2006). *Common formative assessments: How to connect standards-based instruction and assessment.* Thousand Oaks, CA: Corwin Press.

Bangert-Drowns, R. L., Hurley, M. M., & Wilkinson, B. (2004). The effects of school-based writing-to-learn interventions on academic achievement: A meta-analysis. *Review of Educational Research, 74*(1), 29–58.

Bernhardt, V. L. (2004). *Data analysis for continuous school improvement.* Larchmont, NY: Eye on Education.

Borman, G. D., Benson, J. G., & Overman, L. (2009, March). A randomized field trial of the Fast ForWord language computer-based training program. *Educational Evaluation and Policy Analysis, (31)*1, 82–106.

Bossidy, L., & Charan, R. (2002). *Execution: The discipline of getting things done.* New York: Crown Business.

Carbonneau, N., Vallerand, R. J., Fernet, C., & Guay, F. (2008). The role of passion for teaching in intrapersonal and interpersonal outcomes. *Journal of Educational Psychology, 100*(4), 977–987.

Casciaro, T., & Lobo, M. S. (2005, June 1). Competent jerks, lovable fools, and the formation of social networks. *Harvard Business Review,* 92–91.

Chenoweth, K. (2007). *It's being done.* Boston: Harvard Education Press.

Coleman, J. S., Campbell, E. Q., Hobson, C. F., McPartland, J. M., Mood, A. M., Weinfeld, F. D., & York, R. L. (1966). *Equality of educational opportunity.* Washington, DC: U.S. Government Printing Office.

Colin, C. (2009, July). Eight impassioned suggestions about where to focus stimulus dollars. *Edutopia.* Retrieved July 4, 2009, from http://www.edutopia.org/economic-stimulus-education-funding-interviews.

Collins, J. (2009). *How the mighty fall: And why some companies never give in.* New York: HarperCollins Publishers Inc.

Colvin, G. (2008). *Talent is overrated: What really separates world-class performers from everybody else.* New York: Portfolio.

Cook, W. J. (2004, September). When the smoke clears. *Phi Delta Kappan, 86*(1),73–75, 83.

Coyle, D. (2009). *The talent code: Greatness isn't born. It's grown. Here's how.* New York: Bantam Dell.

Crenshaw, D. (2008). *The myth of multitasking. How "doing it all" gets nothing done.* San Francisco: Jossey-Bass.

Darling-Hammond, L., & Richardson, N. (2009, February). Teaching learning: What matters? *Educational Leadership, 66*(5), 46–55.

Deutchman, A. (2007). *Change or die: The three keys to change at work and in life.* New York: HarperCollins Publishers Inc.

DuFour, R., DuFour, R., & Eaker, R. (2008). *Revisiting professional learning communities at work: New insights for improving schools.* Bloomington, IN: Solution Tree.

DuFour, R., & Marzano, R. J. (2009, February). High-leverage strategies for principal leadership. *Educational Leadership, 66*(5), 62–69.

Easton, L. B. (2008). *Powerful designs for professional learning* (2nd ed.). Oxford, OH: National Staff Development Council.

Ericsson, K. A., Charness, N., Feltovich, P. J., & Hoffman, R. R. (Eds.). (2006). *The Cambridge handbook of expertise and expert performance.* New York: Cambridge University Press.

Fernandez, K. E. (2006). *Clark County School District Study of the Effectiveness of School Improvement Plans (SESIP).* (Technical Report).

Fink, D., & Hargreaves, A. (2006). *Sustainable leadership.* San Francisco: Jossey-Bass.

Fuhrman, S. H., & Elmore, R. F. (Eds.). (2004). *Redesigning accountability systems for education.* New York: Teachers College Press.

Fullan, M. (2005). *Leadership & sustainability: System thinkers in action.* Thousand Oaks, CA: Corwin Press.

Fullan, M. (2008). *The six secrets of change: What the best leaders do to help their organizations survive and thrive.* San Francisco: Jossey-Bass.

Gabriel, J. G. (2005). *How to thrive as a teacher leader.* Alexandria, VA: Association for Supervision and Curriculum Development.

Gallagher, W. (2009). *Rapt: Attention and the focused life.* New York: Penguin Group.

Goldsmith, M., Morgan, H., & Ogg, A. J. (2004). *Leading organizational learning: Harnessing the power of knowledge.* San Francisco: Jossey Bass.

Goleman, D. (2006). *Social intelligence: The new science of human relationships.* New York: Bantam Books.

Goodlad, J. I. (1984). *A place called school: Prospects for the future.* New York: McGraw-Hill.

Graesser, A. C. (2009, May). Inaugural editorial. *Journal of Educational Psychology, 101*(2), 259–261.

Gross, B., Booker, T. K., & Goldhaber, D. (2009, June). Boosting student achievement: The effect of comprehensive school reform on student achievement. *Educational Evaluation and Policy Analysis, 31*(2), 111–126.

Guskey, T. R. (2000). *Evaluating professional development.* Thousand Oaks, CA: Corwin Press.

Hamel, G. (2009, February). Moon shots for management. *Harvard Business Review, 87*(2), 91–98.

Hargreaves, A. (2007). Resourcefulness: Restraint and renewal. In *Jossey-Bass reader on educational leadership* (2nd ed., pp. 445–470). San Francisco: Jossey-Bass.

Hattie, J. (2009). *Visible learning: A synthesis of over 800 meta-analyses relating to achievement.* New York: Routledge.

Haycock, K. (1998, Summer). Good teaching matters ... a lot. *The Education Trust, 3*(2).

Hirsh, S. (2009, Winter). Before deciding what to do, determine what is necessary. *Journal of the National Staff Development Council, 30*(1), 71–72.

Howard, J. (2009). The Efficacy Institute Inc. Message posted to http://www.ncrel.org/sdrs/areas/issues/students/learning/lr2effic.htm.

Ingersoll, R. M., & Perda, D. (2009, March). *The mathematics and science teacher shortage: Fact and myth* (Report #RR-62). Philadelphia: Consortium for Policy Research in Education.

Jansen, J. D. (2009). When politics and emotion meet: Educational change in racially divided communities. In A. Hargreaves & M. Fullan (Eds.), *Change wars* (pp. 185–200). Bloomington, IN: Solution Tree.

Joyce, B. (2004, September). How are professional learning communities created? History has a few messages. *Phi Delta Kappan, 86*(1), 76–83.

Kachigan, S. K. (1986). *Statistical analysis: An interdisciplinary introduction to univariate & multivariate methods.* New York: Radius Press.

Kant, I. (1785, republished 2008). *Groundwork for the metaphysics of morals.* Radford, VA: A&D Publishing.

Kaplan, R. S., & Norton, D. P. (1996). *The balanced scorecard: Translating strategy into action*. Boston: Harvard Business School Press.

Kaplan, R. S., & Norton, D. P. (2000). *The strategy-focused organization: How balanced scorecard companies thrive in the new business environment*. Boston: Harvard Business School Publishing Corp.

Kaufman, R. (1995). *Mapping educational success: Strategic thinking and planning for school administrators*. Thousand Oaks, CA: Corwin Press.

Kim, W. C., & Mauborgne, R. (2003, January). Fair process: Managing in the knowledge economy. *Harvard Business Review, 81*(1), 127–136.

Kiuhara, S. A., Graham, S., & Hawken, L. S. (2009, February). Teaching writing to high school students: A national survey. *Journal of Educational Psychology, 101*(1), 136–160.

Liptak, A. (2009, June 26). Supreme Court says child's rights violated by strip search. *New York Times*. Retrieved July 3, 2009, from http://www.nytimes.com/2009/06/26/us/politics/26scotus.html.

Loehr, J., & Schwartz, T. (2003). *The power of full engagement: Managing energy, not time, is the key to high performance and personal renewal*. New York: Free Press.

Marshall, K. (2010). *Rethinking teacher supervision and evaluation: How to work smart, build collaboration, and close the achievement gap*. San Francisco: Jossey-Bass.

Marzano, R. J. (2001). *Designing a new taxonomy of educational objectives*. Thousand Oaks, CA: Corwin Press.

Marzano, R. J. (2007). *The art and science of teaching: A comprehensive framework for effective instruction*. Alexandria, VA: Association for Supervision and Curriculum Development.

Marzano, R. J., & Waters, T. W. (2009). *District leadership that works: Striking the right balance*. Bloomington, IN: Solution Tree.

Marzano, R. J., Waters, T., & McNulty, B. A. (2005). *School leadership that works: From research to results*. Alexandria, VA: Association for Supervision and Curriculum Development.

McFadden, L. (2009, April). District learning tied to student learning. *Phi Delta Kappan, 90*(8), 545–553.

McGuffey, W. H. (1879/1997). *McGuffey's fourth eclectic reader* (rev. ed.). New York: John Wiley & Sons.

Mizell, H. (2009a, May). Delve into NSDC's new definition of professional learning. *The Learning System, 4*(8), 2. Retrieved July 6, 2009, from http://www.nsdc.org/news/getDocument.cfm?articleID=1886.

Mizell, H. (2009b, June 22). Ineffective PD often part of the problem in low-performing schools. Message posted to http://www.nsdc.org/learningBlog/post.cfm/ineffecticve-pd-often-part-of-the-problem-in-low-performing-schools.

Mizell, H. (2009c, July 1). PD or not PD? Constructing a professional development taxonomy. Message posted to http://www.nsdc.org/learningBlog/post.cfm/pd-or-not-pd-judgin-six-activities.

National Staff Development Council. (2009). *Standards for staff development.* Retrieved October 13, 2009, from http://www.nsdc.org/standards/index.cfm.

Neff, T. J., & Citrin, J. M. (1999). *Lessons from the top: The search for America's best business leaders.* New York: Doubleday.

Patterson, K., Grenny, J., Maxfield, D., McMillan, R., & Switzler, A. (2008). *Influencer: The power to change anything.* New York: McGraw-Hill.

Pennebaker, R. (2009, August 29). The mediocre multitasker. *New York Times.* Retrieved October 13, 2009, from http://www.nytimes.com/2009/08/30/weekinreview/20pennebaker.html?-r=2&ref-weekinreview.

Pfeffer, J., & Sutton, R. I. (2000). *The knowing-doing gap: How smart companies turn knowledge into action.* Boston: Harvard Business School Press.

Pfeffer, J., & Sutton, R. I. (2006, January). Evidence-based management. *Harvard Business Review, 84*(1).

Popham, W. J. (2008). *Transformative assessment.* Alexandria, VA: Association for Supervision and Curriculum Development.

Reeves, D. B. (2002a). *The daily disciplines of leadership: How to improve student achievement, staff motivation, and personal organization.* San Francisco: Jossey-Bass.

Reeves, D. B. (2002b, May 8). Galileo's dilemma: The illusion of scientific certainty in educational research. *Education Week, 21*(34), 33, 44.

Reeves, D. B. (2002c). *Making standards work: How to implement standards-based assessments in the classroom, school, and district* (3rd ed.). Denver, CO: Advanced Learning Press.

Reeves, D. B. (2004a). *Accountability for learning: How teachers and school leaders can take charge.* Alexandria, VA: Association for Supervision and Curriculum Development.

Reeves, D. B. (2004b). *Accountability in action: A blueprint for learning organizations* (2nd ed.). Englewood, CO: Advanced Learning Press.

Reeves, D. B. (2006a). *Data for learning: A blueprint for improving student achievement using data teams* [DVD]. Englewood, CO: Advanced Learning Press.

Reeves, D. B. (2006b). *The learning leader: How to focus school improvement for better results.* Alexandria, VA: Association for Supervision and Curriculum Development.

Reeves, D. B. (2006c). Pull the weeds before you plant the flowers. *Educational Leadership, 64*(1), 89–90.

Reeves, D. B. (2008). *Reframing teacher leadership to improve your school.* Alexandria, VA: Association for Supervision and Curriculum Development.

Reeves, D. B. (2009a). *Assessing educational leaders: Evaluating performance for improved individual and organizational results* (2nd ed.). Thousand Oaks, CA: Corwin Press.

Reeves, D. B. (2009b). *Leading change in your school: How to conquer myths, build commitment, and get results.* Alexandria, VA: Association for Supervision and Curriculum Development.

Reeves, D. B. (2009c). Level-five networks: Making significant change in complex organizations. In A. Hargreaves & M. Fullan (Eds.), *Change wars* (pp. 237–258). Bloomington, IN: Solution Tree.

Reeves, D. B., & Allison, E. (2009). *Renewal coaching: Sustainable change for individuals and organizations.* San Francisco: Jossey-Bass.

Rothstein, R. (2004). *Class and schools: Using social, economic, and educational reform to close the black-white achievement gap.* Washington, DC: Economic Policy Institute.

Schmoker, M. J. (2004, February). Tipping point: From feckless reform to substantive instructional improvement. *Phi Delta Kappan, 85*(6), 424–432.

Sharratt, L., & Fullan, M. (2009). *Realization: The change imperative for deepening district-wide reform.* Thousand Oaks, CA: Corwin Press.

Shorter Oxford English dictionary (5th ed.). (2002). New York: Oxford University Press.

Stiggins, R. J. (2007). *Introduction to student-involved assessment for learning* (5th ed.). Upper Saddle River, NJ: Prentice Hall.

Stiggins, R. J., Arter, J., Chappuis J., & Chappuis, S. (2004). *Classroom assessment for student learning: Doing it right, using it well.* Portland, OR: Assessment Training Institute.

Stigler, J. W., & Hiebert, J. (1999). *The teaching gap: Best ideas from the world's teachers for improving education in the classroom.* New York: Free Press.

Sutton, R. I. (2007). *The no asshole rule: Building a civilized workplace and surviving one that isn't.* New York: Warner Business.

Wei, R. C., Darling-Hammond, L., Andree, A., Richardson, N., & Orphanos, S. (2009). *Professional learning in the learning profession: A status report on teacher development in the United States and abroad.* Dallas, TX. National Staff Development Council.

White, S. (2005). *Show me the proof! Tools and strategies to make data work for you.* Englewood, CO: Advanced Learning Press.

White, S. (2009). *Leadership maps.* Englewood, CO: Lead + Learn Press.

Wiggins, G. (1998). *Educative assessment: Designing assessments to inform and improve student performance.* San Francisco: Jossey-Bass.

Wiggins, G., & McTighe, J. (2005). *Understanding by design* (2nd ed.). Alexandria, VA: Association for Supervision and Curriculum Development.

Wiliam, D. (2007). Content *then* process: Teacher learning communities in the service of formative assessment. In D. Reeves (Ed.), *Ahead of the curve: The power of assessment to transform teaching and learning* (pp. 183–206). Bloomington, IN: Solution Tree.

Willingham, D. T. (2009). *Why don't students like school? A cognitive scientist answers questions about how the mind works and what it means for the classroom.* San Francisco: Jossey-Bass.

Yun, J. T., & Moreno, J. F. (2006, January–February). College access, K–12 concentrated disadvantage, and the next 25 years of education research. *Educational Researcher, 35*(1), 12–19.

INDEX

Note: Information presented in figures is denoted by *f.*

ABOUT THE AUTHOR

Douglas B. Reeves is the founder of The Leadership and Learning Center. He has worked with education, business, nonprofit, and government organizations throughout the world. Dr. Reeves is the author of many articles and more than 20 books on leadership and organizational effectiveness, including the ASCD publications *Accountability for Learning: How Teachers and School Leaders Can Take Charge* (2004), *The Learning Leader: How to Focus School Improvement for Better Results* (2006), *Reframing Teacher Leadership to Improve Your School* (2008), and *Leading Change in Your School: How to Conquer Myths, Build Commitment, and Get Results* (2009). He has twice been named to the Harvard University Distinguished Author Series, and he was named the Brock International Laureate for his contributions to education. He also has received the Distinguished Service Award from the National Association of Secondary School Principals and the Parents Choice Award for his writing for children and parents.

Related ASCD Resources: Professional Development

At the time of publication, the following ASCD resources were available (ASCD stock numbers appear in parentheses). For up-to-date information about ASCD resources, go to www.ascd.org.

Multimedia

Creating the Capacity for Change: An ASCD Action Tool by Jody Mason West-brook and Valarie Spisder-Albert (#702118)

Guiding School Improvement with Action Research Books-in-Action Package (10 Books and 1 video) (#700261)

Making School Improvement Happen with What Works in Schools: An ASCD Action Tool Set (Three Tools) by John L. Brown (#705055)

Schooling by Design: An ASCD Action Tool (#707039)

Networks

Visit the ASCD Web site (www.ascd.org) and click on About ASCD. Go to the section on Networks for information about professional educators who have formed groups around topics such as "Restructuring Schools." Look in the Network Directory for current facilitators' addresses and phone numbers.

Online Courses

Visit the ASCD Web site (www.ascd.org) for the following professional development opportunities:

Contemporary School Leadership by Vera Blake (#PD04OC38)

Creating and Sustaining Professional Learning Communities by Vera Blake and Diane Jackson (#PD04OC43)

What Works in Schools: An Introduction by John Brown (#PD04OC36)

Print Products

Accountability for Learning: How Teachers and School Leaders Can Take Charge by Douglas B. Reeves (#104004)

Align the Design: A Blueprint for School Improvement by Nancy J. Mooney and Ann T. Mausbach (#108005)

Connecting Leadership with Learning: A Framework for Reflection, Planning, and Action by Michael Copland and Michael Knapp (#105003)

Enhancing Student Achievement: A Framework for School Improvement by Charlotte Danielson (#102109)

How to Help Your School Thrive Without Breaking the Bank by John G. Gabriel and Paul C. Farmer (#107042)

The Learning Leader: How to Focus School Improvement for Better Results by Douglas B. Reeves (#105151)

The Results Fieldbook: Practical Strategies from Dramatically Improved Schools by Mike Schmoker (#101001)

Transforming Schools: Creating a Culture of Continuous Improvement by Allison Zmuda, Robert Kuklis, and Everett Kline (#103112)

Video and DVD

What Works in Schools (DVD and Facilitator's Guide) (#603047)

Leadership Strategies for Principals (DVD and *The New Principal's Fieldbook: Strategies for Success* by Pam Robbins and Harvey Alvy) (#608033)

The Results Video Series (DVD and Online Facilitator's Guide) (#601261)

A Visit to a Data-Driven School District (DVD and Viewer's Guide) (#606059)

The Whole Child Initiative helps schools and communities create learning environments that allow students to be healthy, safe, engaged, supported, and challenged. To learn more about other books and resources that relate to the whole child, visit www.wholechildeducation.org.

For more information, visit us on the World Wide Web (http://www.ascd.org); send an e-mail message to member@ascd.org; call the ASCD Service Center (1-800-933-ASCD or 703-578-9600, then press 2); send a fax to 703-575-5400; or write to Information Services, ASCD, 1703 N. Beauregard St., Alexandria, VA 22311-1714 USA.